T0185605

SpringerBriefs present concise summaries of cutting-edge research and practical applications across a wide spectrum of fields. Featuring compact volumes of 50 to 125 pages, the series covers a range of content from professional to academic.

Typical publications can be:

- A timely report of state-of-the art methods
- An introduction to or a manual for the application of mathematical or computer techniques
- A bridge between new research results, as published in journal articles
- A snapshot of a hot or emerging topic
- An in-depth case study
- A presentation of core concepts that students must understand in order to make independent contributions

SpringerBriefs are characterized by fast, global electronic dissemination, standard publishing contracts, standardized manuscript preparation and formatting guidelines, and expedited production schedules.

On the one hand, **SpringerBriefs in Applied Sciences and Technology** are devoted to the publication of fundamentals and applications within the different classical engineering disciplines as well as in interdisciplinary fields that recently emerged between these areas. On the other hand, as the boundary separating fundamental research and applied technology is more and more dissolving, this series is particularly open to trans-disciplinary topics between fundamental science and engineering.

Indexed by EI-Compendex, SCOPUS and Springerlink.

More information about this series at http://www.springer.com/series/8884

António Gusmão · Nuno Horta ·
Nuno Lourenço · Ricardo Martins

Analog IC Placement Generation via Neural Networks from Unlabeled Data

 Springer

António Gusmão 🆔
Instituto de Telecomunicações
Lisbon, Portugal

Nuno Lourenço 🆔
Instituto de Telecomunicações
Lisbon, Portugal

Nuno Horta 🆔
Instituto Superior Técnico
Instituto de Telecomunicações
Lisbon, Portugal

Ricardo Martins 🆔
Instituto de Telecomunicações
Lisbon, Portugal

ISSN 2191-530X   ISSN 2191-5318 (electronic)
SpringerBriefs in Applied Sciences and Technology
ISBN 978-3-030-50060-3   ISBN 978-3-030-50061-0   (eBook)
https://doi.org/10.1007/978-3-030-50061-0

© The Author(s), under exclusive license to Springer Nature Switzerland AG 2020
This work is subject to copyright. All rights are solely and exclusively licensed by the Publisher, whether the whole or part of the material is concerned, specifically the rights of translation, reprinting, reuse of illustrations, recitation, broadcasting, reproduction on microfilms or in any other physical way, and transmission or information storage and retrieval, electronic adaptation, computer software, or by similar or dissimilar methodology now known or hereafter developed.
The use of general descriptive names, registered names, trademarks, service marks, etc. in this publication does not imply, even in the absence of a specific statement, that such names are exempt from the relevant protective laws and regulations and therefore free for general use.
The publisher, the authors and the editors are safe to assume that the advice and information in this book are believed to be true and accurate at the date of publication. Neither the publisher nor the authors or the editors give a warranty, express or implied, with respect to the material contained herein or for any errors or omissions that may have been made. The publisher remains neutral with regard to jurisdictional claims in published maps and institutional affiliations.

This Springer imprint is published by the registered company Springer Nature Switzerland AG
The registered company address is: Gewerbestrasse 11, 6330 Cham, Switzerland

To all my friends
—António Gusmão

To Carla, João and Tiago
—Nuno Horta

To Alina, Íris and Ana
—Nuno Lourenço

To Daniela and Martim
—Ricardo Martins

Preface

The proliferation of electronic devices in recent years has triggered the increasing complexity of integrated circuits (ICs). While most of these electronics' high-level functions are implemented using digital circuitry, analog and mixed signal (AMS) circuits are still necessary and irreplaceable in the implementation of most interfaces and transceivers due to the inherent analog nature of those functionalities. While in digital design, an automated flow is well established, for AMS ICs the absence of effective and established computer-aided-design (CAD) tools for electronic design automation (EDA) poses the largest contribution to their bulky development cycles. To address this, long, iterative and error-prone designer intervention over the entire design flow is mandatory. Given the economic pressure for high-quality yet cheap electronics and challenging time-to-market constraints, there is an urgent need for EDA tools that increase the analog designers' productivity and improve the quality of resulting ICs.

In this book, an innovative approach to automate the placement task of analog IC layout design is presented, where artificial neural networks (ANNs) are trained to produce valid layouts at pushbutton speed. Standard ANN applications usually exploit the model's capability of describing a complex, harder to describe, relation between input and target data. For that purpose, ANNs are a mechanism to bypass the process of describing the complex underlying relations between data, by feeding it with a great number of previously acquired input/output data pairs that then the model attempts to copy. However, in the context of analog IC placement generation, the issue arises during the stages of data acquisition, since due to the complexity of the current placement generation flow, output data or labels are very costly to produce, i.e., producing output data in the form of a placement solution for a given input data (a specific circuit topology) is time consuming, and also, the production of a variety of these labels required for the usual neural network application is unrealistic. Therefore, a different approach is taken, since it is quite costly to produce the needed amount of target placements but it is not as complex to describe the relation that makes a placement robust, the model is trained to produce placements that fulfill the defined input/output data relation. The encoded relations are current-flow and symmetry constraints, that, according to analog IC designers, are the most elementary and essential constraints to be considered. In this approach, the system relies on a mix of labeled and unlabeled data that consists of previously designed circuit topologies at sizing-level only, which are easier to obtain.

This book details the description of the input/output data relation that should be fulfilled. The developed description is mainly reflected in two of the system's characteristics, the shape of the input data and the minimized loss function. An efficient modulation of these components should be such that once fully trained, the model should be producing output data that fulfills the desired relation for the given training data, additionally, the model should be capable of efficiently generalizing the acquired knowledge for new examples, i.e., never seen input circuit topologies. In order to address the latter, an abstract and segmented description of both the input data and the objective behavior are developed so the model can identify, in new scenarios, sub-blocks found in the training data. The result is a device level description of the input topology focusing, for each device, on describing its relation to every other device in the topology. Through this description, an unfamiliar overall topology can be decomposed into devices subject to the same constraints as a device in one of the training topologies. Similarly, the desired relation encoded in the loss function directly quantifies the degree to which these device level constraints are being satisfied along with some optimization metrics, such as layout area or device overlap (both being minimized).

The trained ANNs are demonstrated to produce a variety of valid placement solutions even outside the scope of the seen training/validation sets, showing that the model is effectively identifying common components between newer topologies and reutilizing the acquired knowledge. Ultimately, the used methodology efficiently adapts to the given problem's context (high label production cost) and results in an efficient, inexpensive and fast model.

This book is organized into six chapters.

Chapter 1 gives an introduction to AMS systems-on-chip (SoC) design, with special focus given to automatic device placement in analog IC layout generation and the limitations that the current design flow faces. The standard procedures are presented. Furthermore, the concept of machine learning (ML) and the use of this branch of artificial intelligence (AI) as a step towards the production of EDA tools for analog and mixed signal ICs is introduced.

Chapter 2 thoroughly studies ANNs through the deconstruction of the ML model. Its several parts are described, and a comparison of the different used methods for each of these components is made, such as the functioning of each neuron, the learning process that makes use of optimization tools, the hyperparameters that define the model's architecture, and the influence of the selected features.

Chapter 3 explains the constraints which influence the process of layout generation, along with the description of four main approaches of existing EDA tools for analog placement/for analog IC layout.

Chapter 4 details the envisioned solution based on a past approach that is limited to a single circuit topology and punishes valid, innovative predictions. Attention is put into the development of the input features that expand the solution's scope and increase generalization, and, the introduction of a new loss function that evaluates the prediction made through the fulfillment of the circuit's topological constraints.

Chapter 5 details the tests and analysis performed on the different ANN models. These models differ by the format of their input vector or by the loss function used during training, while the network's architecture is kept the same. The objective is to compare the impact of these key parts of the model.

Chapter 6 presents the conclusions of this book, as well as future directions for further applications of ANNs towards the automation of the placement process of analog IC layout design.

The work described in this book was funded by FCT/MCTES through national funds and when applicable co-funded EU funds under the project UIDB/EEA/50008/2020. Including internal research project LAY(RF)^2.

Lisbon, Portugal

António Gusmão
Nuno Horta
Nuno Lourenço
Ricardo Martins

Contents

Acronyms

AI	Artificial Intelligence
AMS	Analog and Mixed-Signal
ANN	Artificial Neural Networks
CAD	Computer Aided Design
CFSSA	Cascode Free Single Stage Amplifier
EDA	Electronic Design Automation
FSSA	Folded Single Stage Amplifier
IC	Integrated Circuit
ML	Machine Learning
MSE	Mean Squared Error
MSE-NP	Mean Squared Error—Non Polynomial Features
MSE-NPS	Mean Squared Error—Non Polynomial Features with Device Scrambling
MSE-P	Mean Squared Error—Polynomial Features
MSE-PS	Mean Squared Error—Polynomial Features with Device Scrambling
TLF	Topological Loss Function
SoC	Systems-on-Chip
SSA	Single Stage Amplifier

Chapter 1
Introduction

1.1 Mixed-Signal Systems-on-Chip Paradigm

Integrated circuits (ICs) are a major driving factor for unleashing the innovative potential of digitizing the industry, society, and every day's life. The semiconductors and systems market is expected to continue to grow at an annual rate of almost 7% over the next 5 years and the analog components market in all semiconductor segments is expected to grow until 2023 with a CAGR of 7.4%. The design of such complex multi-million transistors ICs is only possible due to the use of computer aided design (CAD) and electronic design automation (EDA) tools that support the design process. However, the lack of automation tools prevents effective analog and mixed-signal (AMS) IC design and reuse, and creates barriers for the development of the ICs needed for more energy-efficient and smaller Internet-of-Things, Smart Sensor or Wearable Electronic devices.

As AMS ICs are difficult to design and reuse, designers have been replacing analog circuits by digital computing, however analog circuitry is needed to interface with the real world as some functionalities are inherently analog (e.g. sensing a system's inputs like the signals from a microphone). As a result, a lot of real world implementations are the result of a mix between digital (used in most of the high level functions) and analog circuits. While in most of these AMS systems on chip (SoC) the area occupied by the analog components is usually smaller than its digital counterparts, the effort put into their design is typically higher as shown in Fig. 1.1.

Due to this difference in required effort, a lot of research has recently been conducted into the development of new methods and approaches towards the automation of the design process of analog ICs. Despite the considerable evolution of the tools for automatic analog IC design, there is still a long way to go before they reach the level of automation observed in the tools for digital circuit design [1]. Since the CAD tools for EDA have not yet reached the desired level of maturity, human intervention during all stages of the process is mandatory, leading to manual exploration of

© The Author(s), under exclusive license to Springer Nature Switzerland AG 2020
A. Gusmão et al., *Analog IC Placement Generation via Neural Networks from Unlabeled Data*, SpringerBriefs in Applied Sciences and Technology,
https://doi.org/10.1007/978-3-030-50061-0_1

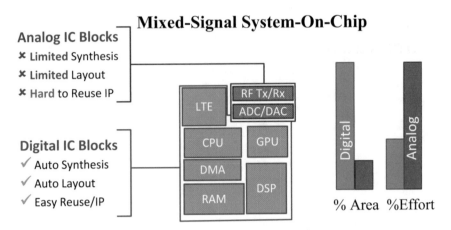

Fig. 1.1 Contrast between Analog and Digital blocks' area of implementation in an AMS SoC and the corresponding effort to implement them from the perspective of a designer [2]

the solution space. The design flow is thus characterized by time-consuming, non-systematic and error-prone interactions between the designer and commonly used CAD tools such as circuit simulators, layout editing environment and verification tools [3]. Meanwhile, the problem is aggravated through the increase in demanded complexity of the systems and technology nodes, resulting in a higher number of transistors which in turn increase the complexity of the design problem by increasing the number of interactions that should be taken into account.

Overall, the difference in difficulty when designing analog ICs can be explained by the: lack of a systematic design flow supported by mature EDA tools; the integration of analog circuits using technology optimized for digital circuits; and, the continuous nature of analog circuit's signals that make them extremely sensible to parasitic disturbances, crosstalk, thermal noise, process variability, aging, device modeling accuracy and layout dependent effects turning the design process very problem specific and greatly restricting the use of previous solutions. As such, there is high demand for analog EDA tools being accompanied with intensive research efforts. Still, no automatic solution for analog IC design matured to be widely used or recognized in the industry. Indicating that there is still long way to go in the making of analog IC design automation solutions that meet designers' needs and increase their productivity.

1.2   Mixed-Signal Design Flow

The design of AMS SoC can be split into seven stages as represented in Fig. 1.2 [4].

1. *Conceptual Design*: The stage where the product is conceptualized, that is, its specifications are gathered and the general product concept is defined.

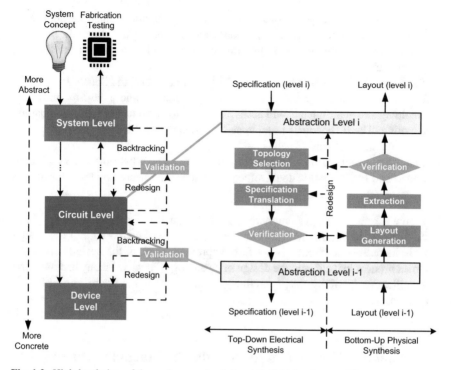

Fig. 1.2 High-level view of the analog or mixed-signal SoC design process [5]

2. *System Design*: In this stage, the overall architecture of the system is designed and partitioned. Hardware and software parts are defined, additionally, interfaces have to be specified. This stage includes decisions on the implementation level, such as package selection and target technology.
3. *Architectural Design*: This stage is concerned with the decomposition of the hardware part in functional blocks (analog and digital), which, when connected, fulfill the specified behavioral specifications. Hardware description languages, such as VHDL or Verilog, are then used to describe the composing blocks, which are ultimately defined by their specifications. Simulations that check whether the specifications, defined in the first stage, are fulfilled or not are then used to test the high-level architecture.
4. *Cell Design*: For analog blocks, a detailed implementation of their components is made. More complex blocks are further decomposed into a set of sub-blocks but ultimately, every block is described by a device-level circuit schematic with the corresponding sizing of the circuit parameters. During the process, manufacturability considerations (tolerances and mismatches) are taken into account in order to guarantee a high yield and/or robustness. The resulting circuit design is tested using SPICE-type circuit simulations.

5. *Cell Layout*: This stage translates the electrical schematic of the different analog blocks into a geometrical representation while minimizing the area of the resulting layout and reducing any parasitics that have a negative impact on the circuit's performance.
6. *System Layout*: The generation of system-level layout of an IC includes system-level block placement and routing, power-grid routing and a description of any shielding and guarding that will act as a measure to prevent crosstalk and substrate coupling. The IC becomes testable and a detailed verification is performed with the embedded software.
7. *Fabrication and Testing*: This is the processing stage where the masks are generated and the ICs fabricated. Defective devices are rejected by tests during and after the fabrication.

Figure 1.2 and its stages enumerate the milestones and requirements that have to be fulfilled during the design of an analog and mixed signal IC, but the design flow, in its entire complexity, is not fully expressed. Each of the design stages is a complex process in itself, and the design of an analog IC involves many backtracking and verification iterations that, even though represented in the figure, appear highly simplified.

1.3   Analog IC Placement Automation by Machine Learning

Currently, a lot of EDA research has been made in an effort to automate the stages of both cell design [6–8] and cell layout [9–11]. This book addresses a task in the cell layout stage, specifically the placement of analog devices on the circuit's layout. For an effective placement, the location of the devices must follow several constraints. Symmetry, matching and current flow-aware placement (addressed in this book) are some of the most important to take into account in order to minimize the impact of the layout in the circuit's desired performance. It is possible to distinguish four other constraints that should be taken into account during the development of the layout, i.e., common centroid, regularity, boundary and grouping [9] resulting in a complex problem of multiple interconnected dependencies.

Established approaches in the development of EDA tools towards analog IC layout generation could be split into three main categories differentiated by the amount of previously existing solutions (commonly denoted as legacy designs or legacy layouts) used as reference during the process of generating a new solution [12]. Layout generation considering placement and routing constraints (without considering legacy designs), layout migration and retargeting from a previous legacy design or template, and layout synthesis with knowledge mining from multiple previously designed layouts. In practice, the different approaches all have the objective of fulfilling the eight constraints aforementioned and diverge on whether they do it explicitly (when no legacy layout is considered) or indirectly through the use of pre-existing solutions that fulfill these constraints and as such have the knowledge of the original designer embedded into them. However, the recent development in artificial intelligence (AI) and machine learning (ML) methods, and available computational capabilities can be used to forge new approaches for the automation of analog IC placement making viable a fourth methodology, in addition to the three others already presented.

ML is the process through which a computer improves its capabilities by the analysis of past experiences. It is now commonly accepted by developers of AI systems that, for a vast number of applications, training a system by either showing it examples of desired input-output behavior or by rewarding system's (initially) random actions that achieve the desired behavior can be easier to program than to anticipate all possible responses for all of the input space [13]. Nevertheless, the process of automatically improving behaviors through experience can be costly and time consuming, especially when large amounts of data must be interpreted and processed. A variety of techniques have been developed in an effort to optimize the process of pattern detection and, in general, the optimal description of the problem in order to achieve the best results is usually the challenging task itself [14]. Some of the most popular ML models nowadays are artificial neural networks (ANNs) that regained a lot of its once lost popularity due to the increasing computational power and data available, allowing the increasing complexity of the networks that, in a general matter, result in better performance. Some approaches already make use of ML models towards the automation of several of the processes in the analog IC design chain such as reinforcement learning [15] and ANNs [16] applied to device sizing, variational autoencoders for mimicking human guidance in routing problems [17], conditional generative adversarial networks to automatize the process of well generation [18] and ANNs for placement generation [12], the latter of which serves as starting point for this book.

The primary goal of the work described in this book is to accelerate and facilitate the process of analog IC placement through ML methodologies, more specifically, through the use of ANNs. The main contributions of it are listed below:

- Research the use of ANNs towards a push-button speed solution for the development of analog IC placement;
- Create an abstract description of some of the topological constraints of a circuit that can then be expanded to include all the remaining restrictions;
- Develop a versatile model capable of proposing robust placements for circuits with a variety of circuit topologies and number of components;
- Study the possibility of an unconventional loss function that is not dependent on past examples and instead directly evaluates the prediction made in an effort to produce a model more robust that produces novel and better solutions.

In sum, a novel approach to both the network's loss function, by using a fully target independent approach, and the description of the circuit in terms of inter-device relations is experimented to show, as proof of concept, the advantages of such approach.

Chapter 2
Artificial Neural Network Overview

The flexibility of artificial neural networks (ANNs), their adaptability to almost any kind of problem, and their low prediction time, the main goal of the work described in this book, made them the prime choice approach in this work, as well as the fact that they can efficiently infer relations from the input and output data. The main disadvantage of ANNs is that they have a high number of hyperparameters to be tuned.

In this chapter the ANNs behavior and associated processes are explained in detail, as well as their hyperparameters, their influence in the model and the importance of selecting the essential features for the description of the problem.

2.1 General Architecture and Behavior

The central idea behind ANNs is to extract linear combinations of the inputs as derived features, and then model the target as a nonlinear function of these features. ANNs are constituted by a network of interconnected elementary neurons usually forming $2 + n$ layers, an input layer, an output layer, and n hidden layers as shown in Fig. 2.1.

The number of neurons in the input layer matches the number of input features selected. Similarly, the output layer has the same number of neurons as the number of outputs desired. The number of both hidden layers and neurons in each of these is one of the hyperparameters of the model and will be further analyzed in Sect. 2.6, but, in general, a higher number of layers and neurons are capable of inferring more complex relations between the network's input and output for the same number of trainable weights.

© The Author(s), under exclusive license to Springer Nature Switzerland AG 2020

A. Gusmão et al., *Analog IC Placement Generation via Neural Networks from Unlabeled Data*, SpringerBriefs in Applied Sciences and Technology, https://doi.org/10.1007/978-3-030-50061-0_2

Fig. 2.1 An example of an
ANN comprised of an input,
an output and n hidden layers

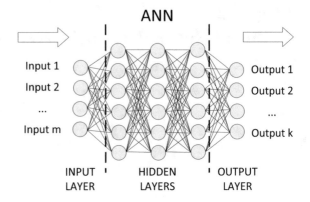

Fig. 2.2 Artificial neuron
overall functioning

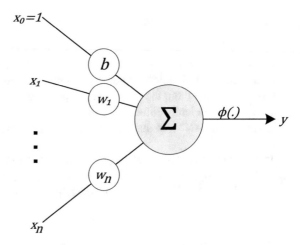

Each of the network's neurons is a function that returns an output y as a function
of its input connections $x_1, \ldots, x_n$ in the form of:

$$y = \phi \left(\sum_{i=1}^{n} (w_i x_i) + b \right), \qquad (2.1)$$

where ϕ is the neuron's activation function, which constitutes another hyperparameter that will be further analyzed in Sect. 2.7, w_i is the linear combination weight
associated to input connection x_i and b indicates the neuron's bias that can be treated
as another weight w_0 associated to a constant input of value $x_0 = 1$ resulting in the
simpler expression:

$$y = \phi \left(\sum_{i=0}^{n} (w_i x_i) \right), \qquad (2.2)$$

visualized in Fig. 2.2.

In fully connected ANNs, for a node in layer j, its inputs are the outputs of all neurons in layer $j - 1$ and its output will be an input for all neuron's in layer $j + 1$. Taking the behavior of each neuron into account and the network's architecture from Fig. 2.1, which is composed by several sequential layers of interconnected neurons, it is possible to interpret that the network's output to any given input is the result of the inputs' propagation through each layer of the network. The output of a given layer j with n neurons preceded by a layer with m neurons can be described as a $\mathbb{R}^m \longrightarrow \mathbb{R}^n$ function where the output of each neuron is given by (2.2). The learning process consists in the iterative adjustment of the network's total neurons' weights so that the network's transformation of inputs into outputs optimizes a certain evaluation metric called the loss function.

In a supervised learning context, to each example used during the learning phase (phase where the objective is to adjust the model's weights as opposed to test phase in which its performance is evaluated), there is a desired output associated, the targets. In these cases, the model's outputs are evaluated in comparison to the given targets through a loss function similar to the mean squared error (MSE) function defined through:

$$MSE = \frac{1}{n} \sum_{i=1}^{n} (Y_i - \hat{Y}_i)^2. \tag{2.3}$$

where Y is the prediction made by the model while $\hat{Y}$ contains the targets. These targets are the human knowledge fed into the system. The MSE loss function is widely used in supervised regression models and encourages the update of the networks weights such that the output is as close as possible to the given targets.

The given targets embed the input/output relation that the designer wishes for the model to learn. Notice however, that several solutions might result in the same MSE loss and translate to significantly different input/output relations as will be shown in Sect. 2.5. In extreme cases, the supplying of targets for every point in the input space would result in the development of the exact desired relation, however this gravely misses the point of the approach as the objective is to easily create a rough approximation of the desired relation by simply feeding to the model some example cases, as opposed to directly describing or even simply inferring this relation in its entirety which constitutes a significantly harder task.

The goal of the model's designer is to define both the loss function and input features in such a way that by giving the available examples as reference, the model is capable of developing a close approximation to the desired relation between input and output that is easy to intuitively precept but hard to materialize and describe.

2.2 Optimizers

The most simple way of updating any model's parameters (which for an ANN are its weights) iteratively in order to minimize a loss function L is through Gradient

Descent [20]. Consider a model with the parameter's vector W of length d. Through the Gradient Descent method, the model's parameters can be updated from iteration t to iteration $t + 1$ through:

$$W_{t+1} = W_t - \eta \nabla L(W_t), \tag{2.4}$$

where η represents the method's parameter, the learning rate. The gradient $\nabla L(W_t)$ gives the direction in the parameter space towards which the loss increases most drastically, as such, the direction $-\nabla L(W_t)$ gives the direction in the parameter space towards which the loss decreases most drastically, therefore the parameters are updated through a step in the direction indicated by $-\nabla L(W_t)$. The learning rate η represents the magnitude of the step taken. However, the magnitude of the step should not overshoot the function's minimum value. If the η value is too large, the model might never converge, or worse, diverge and explode. However, too small steps might take a lot of iterations to converge and makes the model more likely to become stuck in a local minimum of the loss function. Due to this challenge of choosing the correct value η, several new optimizers have been proposed.

One very common concept in more complex methods is the concept of momentum introduced in [21] and it's objective is to simulate the physical sense of acceleration [22]. It takes into account the past gradients and if its direction remains the same. This concept is mathematically encoded through

$$W_{t+1} = W_t - \Delta W_{t+1} \qquad \Delta W_{t+1} = \beta \Delta W_t + \eta \nabla L(W_t), \tag{2.5}$$

where β is usually set to $\beta = 0.9$. Note the recursive nature of the update factor ΔW_{t+1} that depends on the update factors of all previous iterations. The update on the parameters gets bigger as the iterations progress consistently, making it easier to escape from plateaus and local minima of the loss function. When the gradient changes its direction between iterations, the algorithm reduces the step taken as if the parameter update was affected by inertia.

A common issue with the mentioned approaches is that the same learning rate applies to all parameter updates. If the data is sparse and its features have very different frequencies, rarely occurring features should result in a larger parameter update [23]. Adaptive Gradient (AdaGrad) [24] addresses this issue: It adapts the learning rate to the parameters, performing larger updates for infrequent and smaller updates for frequent parameters. For this reason, it is well-suited for dealing with sparse data. As such, the parameter η is now a vector of learning rates H, one for each of the model's d parameters. The values for each of these learning rates also varies in time t. The update of a given i parameter at instance $t + 1$ is defined through:

$$w_{i,t+1} = w_{t,i} - \frac{H}{\sqrt{G_{t,ii} + \epsilon}} \nabla L(w_{t,i}), \tag{2.6}$$

where $G_{t,ii} \in \mathbb{R}^{d \times d}$ is a diagonal matrix where each diagonal element i, i is the sum of the squares of the gradients with respect to w_i up to time step t through:

$$G_{t,ii} = \sum_{j=0}^{t} (\nabla L(w_{j,i}))^2, \tag{2.7}$$

and ϵ is a smoothing term that avoids division by zero (usually in the order of 1×10^{-8}). The added adaptive term from (2.7), decreases the learning rate every time $\nabla L(w_{t,i}) \neq 0$. Thus, more frequent parameters are updated less drastically than less frequent terms. Note that for very frequent parameters, the adaptive term keeps growing until the parameter's update is infinitesimally small and no new knowledge is acquired.

To avoid this accumulation in the adaptive term, some methods like RMSprop associate a decaying term $0 < \gamma < 1$(usually 0.9) to the sum of gradients in order to consider strongly the most recent gradient values [23]. The adaptive term for parameter w_i in instant t is thus defined through:

$$G_{t,ii} = \gamma (\nabla L(w_{t,i}))^2 + (1 - \gamma) G_{t-1,ii}. \tag{2.8}$$

Finally, the Adaptive Moment Estimation (Adam) optimizer [25] mixes both the concept of the gradient's momentum from [21] and its second momentum, seen in the RMSprop, used to adapt the optimizer's learning rate. The gradient's first momentum in instance t is defined as:

$$m_t = \frac{\beta_1 m_{t-1} + (1 - \beta_1) \nabla L(W_t)}{1 - \beta_1}, \tag{2.9}$$

similarly to (2.5) with the addition of a bias-correcting term [23]. The gradient's second momentum is defined as:

$$v_t = \frac{\beta_2 v_{t-1} + (1 - \beta_2)(\nabla L(W_t))^2}{1 - \beta_2} \tag{2.10}$$

similarly to (2.8), again with the addition of a bias-correcting term. Finally the update of the parameters is given by:

$$W_{t+1} = W_t - \frac{\eta}{\sqrt{v_t + \epsilon}} m_t, \tag{2.11}$$

The authors propose default values of 0.9 for β_1, 0.999 for β_2, 10^{-8} for ϵ and 0.001 for η with which it has been shown to perform well in several context [25], reducing the need of adjustment. The adaptive learning rate makes Adam (and the other optimizers that use it) appropriate for sparse input data, while the use of momentum makes it faster to converge and less likely to become stuck in saddle points or local minima [23].

2.3 Batch Size

Consider an ANN that has as loss function the MSE from (2.3), The parameter n represents the number of examples considered in the calculation of the loss. During the training phase, the network's weights are adjusted in order to minimize this loss function. Naturally, one would aim for the minimum MSE error across all of the training examples in order to calculate the loss's gradient $\nabla L(W)$ considering all training examples $n = N$. This is denominated Batch Gradient Descent as a single update of the model's weights requires the calculation of the model's gradients for the whole training set, considering it a single batch of data. Batch Gradient Descent can be very slow and is unfeasible for datasets that do not fit in memory but is certain to converge to the global minimum for convex error surfaces [23].

Stochastic Gradient Descent, in contrast, computes the gradients for a single example at a time (i.e. a batch of size 1). This approach results in frequent, high variance updates that results in erratic and noisy parameter updates. However, this erratic behavior might be somehow beneficial since it enables the optimizer to escape local minima while usually performing faster than Batch Gradient Descent.

Mini-batch gradient descent performs a parameter update for a certain number of training examples $0 < n < N$. This approach reduces the variance of the parameter updates, which can lead to more stable convergence when compared to Stochastic Gradient Descent and faster than Batch Gradient Descent.

As such, the process of choosing the size of the data batch considered in each update can influence the results and the overall performance. Again, optimal batch size varies from problem to problem and usually trial and error through educated guesses is used to determine this hyperparameter's value.

2.4 Backpropagation Algorithm

The learning phase of the model consists in a series of input-prediction iterations, where in each, the predictions made are evaluated via a defined loss function L and the model's parameters (each neuron's weights $\{w_{00}, \ldots, w_{mn}\}$ where w_{ij} denotes the weight i associated to neuron j) are updated in order to minimize this function. In order to ensure that the weights' update results in a smaller error, it is necessary to define the error's derivative in relation to each neuron's weight $\frac{\delta L}{\delta w_{ij}}$. In order to efficiently calculate these gradients, the backpropagation algorithm [26] is used.

Consider a network composed by one input, two output and two hidden layers with a single neuron each as shown in Fig. 2.3. The output for any given neuron of the network is defined in (2.2). Considering a supervised problem where the label associated with a specific example is denominated $\hat{y}$ then the error between the prediction made and the given target might be defined by:

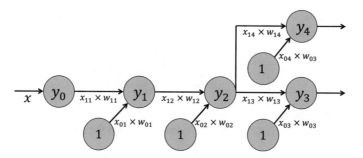

Fig. 2.3 Network consisting of two hidden layers with a single neuron each. The network's parameters consist in its weights w_{ij}, $i \in \{0, 1\}$, $j \in \{1, \ldots, 4\}$. $y = (y_3, y_4)$ is the network's output and x is the network's input

$$L(y, \hat{y}) = \sum_i L_i = \sum_i (y_i - \hat{y}_i)^2, \tag{2.12}$$

where i indexes the dimensions of the produced output and target (2 dimensions in the case presented in Fig. 2.3).

It is possible to split the error between the output's dimensions through:

$$L(y, \hat{y}) = L_3(y_3, \hat{y}_3) + L_4(y_4, \hat{y}_4) \tag{2.13}$$

where L_3 and L_4 correspond to the error associated to y_3 and y_4 respectively, each defined through:

$$L_3(y_3, \hat{y}_3) = (y_3 - \hat{y}_3)^2 \tag{2.14}$$

$$L_4(y_4, \hat{y}_4) = (y_4 - \hat{y}_4)^2 \tag{2.15}$$

Through (2.2), it is possible to define the y_3 output as the result of applying an activation function to the weighted sum of the last neuron's inputs. Replacing in Eq. 2.14:

$$L(\phi_3(z_3), \hat{y}) = (\phi_3(z_3) - \hat{y})^2, \tag{2.16}$$

where ϕ_3 denotes the activation function of the neuron that produces the output y_3 (neuron 3) and z_3 represents the weighted sum of the same neuron's inputs, defined as:

$$z_3 = \sum_{i=0}^{1} (w_{i3} \times x_{i3}), \tag{2.17}$$

where x_{i3} represents the input $i = \{0, 1\}$ to neuron 3. Furthermore, $x_{13} = y_2$ is the output of neuron 2 in the second to last layer of the network, which in turn is one of the inputs for neuron 3. Remember also that w_{03} represents the neuron's bias b_3 that can be represented as a weight associated to a constant input of 1, so the task of updating the biases and the weights is technically the same. So in order to calculate $\frac{\delta L}{\delta w_{i3}}$, one can make use of the chain rule and define the partial derivative as:

$$\frac{\delta L}{\delta w_{i3}} = \frac{\delta L_3}{\delta w_{i3}} = \frac{\delta L_3}{\delta \phi_3} \frac{\delta \phi_3}{\delta z_3} \frac{\delta z_3}{\delta w_{i3}}, \tag{2.18}$$

where note that $\frac{\delta z_3}{\delta w_{i3}} = x_{i3}$, i.e. the input i for node 3 that corresponds to the output of the neurons connected to it, the bias' constant neuron for $i = 0$ and neuron 2's y_2 for $i = 1$.

Note that for this last neuron, no matter the number of inputs it has, the calculation of the loss's partial derivative in relation to any of its n associated weights would be given by Eq. 2.18 with $i = \{0, \ldots, n\}$ denoting the weight associated to its ith input (with 0 being the bias). For neuron 4, the process would be identical, with the influence of the neuron's weights in the calculated loss being given by:

$$\frac{\delta L}{\delta w_{i4}} = \frac{\delta L_4}{\delta w_{i4}} = \frac{\delta L_4}{\delta \phi_4} \frac{\delta \phi_4}{\delta z_4} \frac{\delta z_4}{\delta w_{i4}}, \tag{2.19}$$

Since the output of the neuron in the second to last layer propagates to the two nodes in the next layer, when backtracking the error to neuron 2, it is necessary to account its influence on both dimensions of the output, given by:

$$\frac{\delta L}{\delta w_{i2}} = \sum_{j=3}^{4} \left(\frac{\delta L}{\delta \phi_j} \frac{\delta \phi_j}{\delta z_j} \frac{\delta z_j}{\delta \phi_2} \right) \frac{\delta \phi_2}{\delta z_2} \frac{\delta z_2}{\delta w_{i2}} \tag{2.20}$$

For any other neuron in the second to last layer, the process would be identical (assuming a fully connected architecture), and by considering m neurons in the output layer, one would only need to change the values over which variable j loops through, making it loop through all m output neurons.

This backtracking of the influences in the loss function can be generalized for any number of layers, for any number of neurons in each of them. The important point however, is that all of the involved functions, the neuron's activation function and the loss function, should be **differentiable** (the weighted sum of a neuron's input is inherently differentiable) in order to allow an efficient update of the model's weights in each iteration.

One other simplification made in the example previously analyzed is the fact that only one example was considered. Take the example of the MSE loss function, it consists in averaging the square sum of the difference to the label across all examples. This doesn't change the process however, as $\frac{\delta L}{\delta w_{ikj}}$ for any weight i for the neuron k in layer j is simply the average across **all examples** of the process previously explained. However, this fact underlines the fact that the calculation of each weight's update is directly tied to the number of examples considered, as discussed in Sect. 2.3.

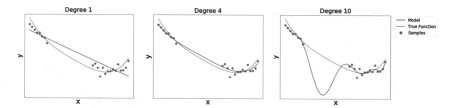

Fig. 2.4 Visualization of the influence of a model's complexity in the overfitting phenomenon. A very simple model is not capable of describing the intricacies of the input/output data relation, however a very complex model creates an unrealistic description of the data. The best model lies somewhere in between [27]

2.5 Regularization

One phenomenon to which machine learning (ML) models are usually subject to is overfitting. A model is said to be overfit if it is too well adjusted to the given training data. A model's goal is usually to modulate a relation between the given input data and output data that, in general, represent real data. Relations between real data are usually not very complex, so the development of a very complex relation to explain the given training data will most likely not describe the real relation existent between the input and output. Figure 2.4 shows a classic example where the excessive complexity of the system results in a perfect fit for the training data, but is completely different from the real relation that generated the data.

One common approach towards evaluating a model's overfit is to reserve some data to test the model during training. By comparing the model's performance in the train and test data, it is possible to assess if the model is overfitting. If the model's error on the test data starts increasing while the error on training data is decreasing, it means that the model is becoming too adjusted to the training data and not generalizing the knowledge to the rest of the input space. Figure 2.5 shows the general relation between these two errors and the model's complexity. The optimum model complexity results in the smaller difference between training and test error as well as minimum values for each.

As the weights are updated in order to minimize the loss function for the given training points, as iterations go on, the model is adjusted to best fit the training data. As a consequence, the training of the model for too many iterations might cause overfit. Early stopping is a regularization technique usually employed that stops the training once the test error begins to increase. Figure 2.6 shows the general relation between training/test error and the number of training iterations. This figure might seem very similar to Fig. 2.5 and it is easy to assume that complexity and number of training iterations are directly related, which to some extent is safe to conclude that they are, however it is not true that in each iteration the network's complexity increases. Early stopping tackles the fact that the model becomes ever more adjusted to the training data as iterations go on and this is true regardless of whether its complexity increases or not.

Fig. 2.5 General relation between training/test error and model complexity [28]

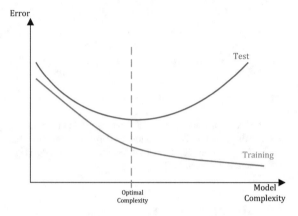

Fig. 2.6 General relation between training/validation error and training iterations (epochs) [29]

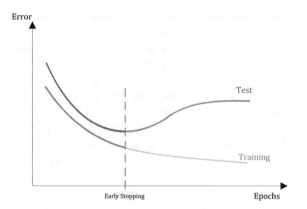

Large network weights result in small variations in the input causing large variations in the output, as such, these describe less smooth relations similarly to the overfitted model in Fig. 2.4. Lasso and Tikhonov Regularization are two techniques that, by adding terms to the loss function, limit the magnitude of the network's weights in order to reduce overfit [30]. Lasso (or $L1$) regularization adds to the loss function a factor that penalizes in accordance to the absolute value of the network's weights, resulting in a loss function defined through:

$$L' = L + \lambda \sum_{i=0}^{n} |w_i|,$$

(2.21)

where L represents the previous loss function, L' the new loss function, n the total number of weights of the network, w_i a given weight of the network and λ an adjustable parameter.

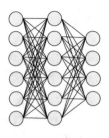
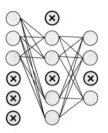

(a) Standard Neural Network   (b) After applying dropout

Fig. 2.7 Standard neural network with and without dropout applied. Crossed units represent dropped out units

Tikhonov (or $L2$) adds a penalizing factor in function of the square of the network's weights through:

$$L' = L + \lambda \sum_{i=0}^{n} w_i^2, \qquad (2.22)$$

By penalizing the square of the weight's values, higher weight values are more heavily penalized by the $L2$ regularization than by $L1$, as such it is said that $L2$ regularization promotes small all around weights. However, $L2$ regularization penalizes with less severity small weights so it is not usual for weights to be driven to zero, whereas $L1$ regularization through a heavier penalization of smaller weights, leads to a higher number of null weights, useful for eliminating any possible useless feature in the input vector.

Dropout [31] is becoming one of the most commonly used regularization techniques used in ANNs, because it addresses two major problems: it prevents overfitting and provides a way of approximately combining different ANN architectures. Dropout is a method that approximates training a large number of neural networks with different architectures in parallel.

During the training of the network, in a given iteration, each neuron is dropped with a probability $1 - p$ where p denotes the neuron's specific independent probability of being kept (usually the same probability is applied to all nodes or to all nodes in a specific layer). Dropping a neuron consists in eliminating it temporarily from the network by eliminating its incoming and outgoing connections. Once the selected nodes are eliminated, the architecture of the network is simpler than its original as shown in Fig. 2.7.

Dropout has the effect of making the training process noisy, forcing nodes within a layer to probabilistically take on more, or less, responsibility for the inputs. This method targets cases where neurons may change in a way that they fix up the mistakes of the other neurons. These cases may lead to complex co-adaptations that in turn lead to overfitting because these co-adaptations do not generalize to unseen data. So by preventing these complex co-adaptations to form, dropout is preventing overfit.

2.6   Hidden Layers and Number of Neurons

As aforementioned and shown in Fig. 2.1, an ANNs architecture is composed by an input and output layer as well as one or more hidden layers. The number of hidden layers greatly influences the complexity of the modeled input/output relation. A larger number of layers describes a more complex relation and tends to lead to better results. However, this increasing complexity might lead to overfitting as just mentioned, and increases the time and computational power required during the training stages. In contrast, a small number of layers might not be capable of accurately modulating the relation between the data. Unfortunately there is no formula in choosing the number of layers in the network and current approaches generally resort to either brute force (preforming a search in the depth space) or revolve around intuition and educated adjustments. The used approach in the development of the models described in this book consists in gradually increasing the number of layers until the results show no further sign of improvement.

Along with the number of layers, one must also consider the number of neurons in each of them. For the input layer, the number of neurons is equal to the number of features considered. Similarly, the number of neurons in the output layer is the same as the expected number of outputs, in this work, an x and y coordinate pair for each device considered. However, the number of neurons in each of the hidden layers is one other hyperparameter that should be tuned. Again, there is no perfect formula to pick the number of neurons in each layer although there are some heuristics such as the ones developed in [32–34]. Ultimately, the optimal solution varies from problem to problem.

One of the simplest methods is through empirical analysis and it works by training the network with different combinations of number of neurons for the hidden layers and save the one that had the best results. The problem with this method is that it is really time consuming since training an ANN usually requires a long time. This work is done on top of the work done in citeguerrasps2019, as such, the initial model was the one used and expanded for the current work. Some pruning techniques can be used after in order to eliminate nodes that, if removed from the network, would not noticeably affect network performance. One pruning technique consists in removing one of the nodes in an edge with weight very close to 0.

2.7   Activation Function

As explained in Sect. 2.1, each neuron's output is determined through Eq. 2.2 where $\phi(z)$ denotes the neuron's activation function that represents one of the hyperparameters of the network. A neuron's activation function is what ultimately defines its behavior and capabilities. As such, non-linear activation functions are usually used, since usually the relation between the data is non-linear. Each of the activation functions researched have their purpose, their strengths and weaknesses, but note that for

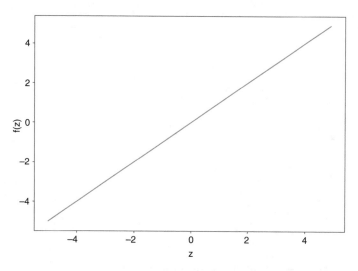

Fig. 2.8 Linear activation function, used in the output layer in regression problems

the backpropagation algorithm to work, each neuron's activation function should be differentiable.

In regression problems the model's output is usually a real value, either negative or positive. Therefore, the output layer nodes' activation function is usually a linear function since its codomain consists in the entire real set. Figure 2.8 shows the function's plot. Concerning the backpropagation algorithm, it's a differentiable function with a simple constant derivative. This constant derivative term constitutes one of the main issues with the linear function (additionally to the fact that it cannot modulate non-linear relations), since no matter the error, it will always contribute with a constant factor to the weight update.

The sigmoid (or logistic activation function) maps the input values to a output range]0, 1[, which essentially encodes their probability of belonging to a certain class making it commonly used in multi-class classification problems, it also prevents cases where its output reaches invalid high values that can happen to unbounded cases such as the linear function. Another attractive aspect of the sigmoid for classification problems is how it has a very steep curve in the vicinities of $z = 0$ as seen in Fig. 2.9, this makes it very sensitive to small variations in this area resulting in a clearer separation of the data. Its gradient is smooth as well which makes it well-behaved during the backpropagation algorithm. Notice, however, how in Fig. 2.9 the function seems to have two asymptotes in the far sides of the input axis (hence its bounded values), in these almost horizontal regions the function is not at all sensitive to changes in the input, i.e. its gradient is very small, approaching 0, which results in a lack of updates for the model's weights, which is the same as it stopping its learning.

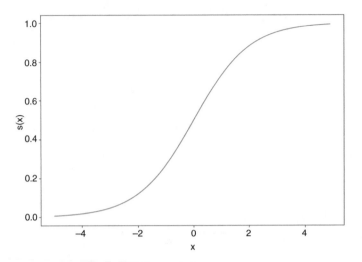

Fig. 2.9 Visual representation of the sigmoid function $S(x)$

The Rectified Linear Unit (ReLU) activation function is computed through $f(z) = max(0, z)$ and its plot is shown in Fig. 2.10, the function's output is 0 if its input is less than or equal to 0, otherwise, its output is equal to its input. Although it might not seem like it, ReLu is nonlinear in nature and is thus able to encode non-linear relations. Its simple formula makes it less computationally heavy than the sigmoid function. Notice however, that the function does not have an upper bound making it susceptible to exploding outputs. However it does address the small vanishing gradients from the sigmoid function, even though it brings up another issue. For the region $z < 0$, the neuron's gradient is 0 and thus it will stop responding to changes in the error. This is called the dying ReLU problem. Another problem arises when its derivative is taken into account since it is not continuous in $z = 0$, these discontinuations make the optimization process more erratic.

In order to address this dying ReLU problem, some variations on the activation function have been introduced such as the Leaky ReLU [35]. However, the most notable is the Exponential Linear Unit (ELU), proposed in [36], whose plot is seen in Fig. 2.11 and its output is determined through:

$$f(z) = \begin{cases} \alpha(e^z - 1) & \text{if } z \le 0 \\ z & \text{if } z > 0, \end{cases} \qquad (2.23)$$

where α is a parameter in itself. This variation solves the dying ReLU issue and has a smooth derivative given by:

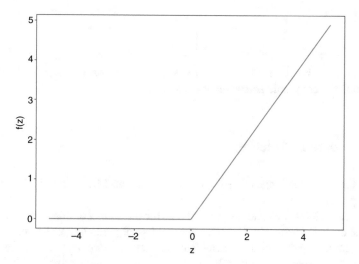

Fig. 2.10   Plot of the Rectified Linear Unit function

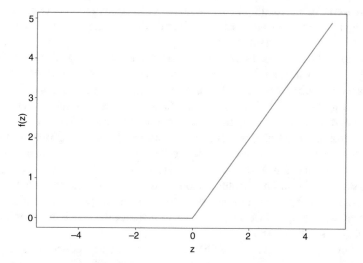

Fig. 2.11   Plot of the Exponential Linear Unit function

$$f(z) = \begin{cases} \alpha e^z & \text{if } z < 0 \\ 1 & \text{if } z > 0. \end{cases}$$

(2.24)

Note that as z approaches 0, the ELU's derivative approaches 1 ensuring that the function is differentiable across the input space.

2.8 Feature Engineering

One of the main challenges faced when developing an ML system, is the selection of the optimal features and its preprocessing.

The selected features should be such that for the same combination of features, the same output is expected. Consider the problem of predicting California Housing Prices from [37]. Some of the dataset features include, for each house in the dataset (which constitute each example), latitude, longitude and total number of rooms. If a model was trained using only latitude and total number of rooms as features, the same combination of values for the pair of features would not have the same expected output (assuming all examples were used) since intuitively, one knows that the longitude of the house's location will likely influence its price, i.e. the loss function (which would most certainly be calculated through comparison between the prediction made and the target value) varies along the longitude feature axis. However, if only these two features were available, the model would be feasible if all houses in the dataset had the same longitude value. That is, in order to ensure a capable model, by reducing the number of features, one should reduce the scope of the solution accordingly. This can be interpreted as forcibly reducing the variability of one of the problem's features through the reduction of the solution's scope. This example might seem trivial at first but it serves as an example for these two factors that should be taken into account, that the same combination of features should have the same expected output and that in order to reduce the number of necessary features, the scope of the solution should be reduced accordingly, inversely, in order to increase the scope of the solution, it might be necessary to add features.

Note however, that it is also possible to feed to the model redundant features that may contribute to an unnecessary complex system and affect its accuracy and overall quality. Features are said to be redundant if they appear to be highly correlated. Consider two features A and B, these are said to be correlated if the values for B can be estimated through the values of A and vice-versa. This existing correlation makes one of the features useless since it is not adding any new information to the system and is instead just adding one additional dimension making the feature space larger than necessary, making the extrapolation of the acquired knowledge a harder task and making the model more complex in the process. Note, however, that existing correlation between two features does not necessarily imply any physical relation between them. Again, this analysis greatly depends on the scope of the developed model and the considered data, two features used in the California Housing Prices dataset might be highly correlated but not for the Alabama Housing Prices for example, or the West Coast Housing Prices. As such, a correlation analysis of the acquired data is of paramount importance in order to properly select only the necessary features for maximum model performance. One generally used technique to reduce data dimensionality is the Principal Component Analysis [38] that transforms a set of observations of possibly correlated features into a set of linearly uncorrelated variables. If the original features were highly correlated, then likely one of the synthetic features can be safely removed as it will have very small variability.

Consider again the California Housing Prices prediction. The latitude feature enables the modulation of the housing prices along the meridians of the map, while the longitude feature does the same for the parallels. However, a synthetic feature *latitude × longitude* would enable the division of the space in a grid like manner, distinguishing examples by the combination of these two features. This is called feature crossing and can provide predictive abilities beyond what those features can provide individually. Polynomial features of degree n consist in crossing features to produce crossings of degree n. For example, if the model's input features were $[a, b, c]$ then its polynomial features of degree $n = 2$ would be $[a, ab, ac, a^2, b, bc, b^2, c, c^2]$. Note that from the added features, only $[ab, ac, bc]$ were a product of actually crossing features.

The scale and distribution of the data drawn from the domain may be different for each variable, for example input variables may have different units (e.g. kilometers, hours, milligrams) likely meaning that the variables have different scales. These variations in scale may cause the network to learn large weight values, which, as aforementioned, may lead to high sensitivity to input variations that may lead to overfitting. Large scale values as targets may lead to large gradient values during backpropagation that may result in an unstable optimization process. In order to avoid both these issues, both input features and targets should have the same scale and be relatively small (around the interval $[-1, 1]$), which can be done through scaling methods such as min-max normalization and standardization.

Min-max normalization scales the range of a given unscaled feature x to the range $[0, 1]$. A scaled version of the feature x' can be determined through:

$$x' = \frac{x - min(x)}{max(x) - min(x)}. \tag{2.25}$$

Standardization models a feature's data as a normal distribution with centered in 0 and standard deviation unitary. It does so through:

$$x' = \frac{x - \mu}{\sigma} \tag{2.26}$$

where μ is the mean of the unscaled feature data and σ its standard deviation.

Categorical features are those that take discrete values, such as *year of birth* or *name*. Take the example of the feature *name*, in order to be interpreted by the computer, it has to be converted into a numerical representation. One intuitive approach is to model the *name* categories similarly to *year of birth*, assign to each possible name an integer. This is called Ordinal Encoding [39] and even though it is very simple, it naturally implies an order and distance between the possible categories [40], i.e. if *Alice* is assigned to 1, *Paul* to 2 and *David* to 3, then *Paul* would be encoded as more similar to *Alice* than *David* is, and *David* would be encoded as more important than both *Alice* and *David*. In this case there is no natural order or similarity between names since semantically no name is closer to another (no distance) nor is it more important than another (no order). One Hot Encoding is the most widely used coding scheme nowadays. It expands the feature into a vector of length equal to the number of possible categories, each of which is assigned to a specific position in the vector. As such, after the conversion the vector is 0 in all positions except for the assigned position for the categorical feature value that is 1. In reality this "vector" is simply the result of creating multiple new features (one for each vector element). This might highly increase the number of features considered if the number of possible categories is very large. Even though the ordinal coding does not expand the number of features, One Hot Encoding has been shown to produce better results [39]. As such, naturally numeric categorical features such as the *year of birth* should also be converted to One Hot Encoding.

2.9 Conclusions

In this chapter, the ANNs' learning process was deconstructed and the most influencing hyperparameters were analyzed and its impact explained.

The process of weight update that constitutes the actual adaptability or learning of the network is based on the backpropagation algorithm that relies on the differentiability of both each neuron's activation function and the model's loss function. However, what dictates each weights' update is ultimately the chosen optimizer. By analyzing the different optimizers, its several components and which problems each addresses, one becomes aware of the challenges of global convergence. Therefore, it is part of the developer's job to not only chose the appropriate optimizer but also to design a well-behaved loss function that attempts to minimize any possible challenges during the convergence phase such as designing a continuous, smooth loss function while also avoiding any possible plateaus. In practice it is not possible to completely have control over the entire shape and behavior of the loss function due to the enormous scale of the parameter space, however these should be nevertheless taken into account and obvious scenarios should be avoided.

Finally, the importance of the chosen representation for the problem's features was analyzed. As previously mentioned, the work detailed in this book expands the scope of the solution developed in [12] to produce a model capable of developing placements for a variety of topologies. As such, the problem's features should be expanded as well in order to properly distinguish between topologies. However, the added information should be optimally added, adding only the necessary information about each problem's example and not any more since this might gravely affect the learning process.

Chapter 3
State-of-the-Art in Analog Integrated Circuit Placement

Determining the location of each device or device group in the actual layout is one of the most critical steps in analog layout synthesis due to all of the constraints that should be taken into account. Furthermore, since the placement task precedes the routing generation, most of parasitic effects and consequent post-layout circuit's performance degradation are established once a placement is fixed. In this chapter, the constraints that should be taken into account during the development of the placement are described in detail, additionally, the two different approaches to represent a placement on an automatic tool are described, as well as their strengths and weaknesses. Finally, the established approaches to automatic placement generation will be categorized and analyzed comparatively.

3.1 Placement Constraints

To keep the performance degradation in check when designing the circuit's layout, a multitude of good practices and design rules must be taken into account. In addition to foundry design rules, recent studies report eight constraints that must be taken into account during the development of an analog integrated circuit (IC) placement [9]:

1. *Symmetry*: A symmetry constraint can affect either a single device, a pair of devices or a group of them as represented in Fig. 3.1. It states that the centroid of the involved devices should be placed along a symmetry axis. This reduces the effect of parasitic mismatches as well as the circuit's sensitivity to process variations. This constraint is especially important when considering differential signals that are sensitive to the mismatch between devices. By following a symmetric approach, the two considered devices in a differential pair (for example) are subject to approximately the same parasitics, thus minimizing their mismatch;

© The Author(s), under exclusive license to Springer Nature Switzerland AG 2020
A. Gusmão et al., *Analog IC Placement Generation via Neural Networks from Unlabeled Data*, SpringerBriefs in Applied Sciences and Technology, https://doi.org/10.1007/978-3-030-50061-0_3

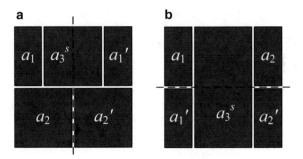

Fig. 3.1 Two types of symmetry composed by symmetric pairs and self-symmetric devices. **a** Symmetric placement along the vertical axis. **b** Symmetric placement along the horizontal axis

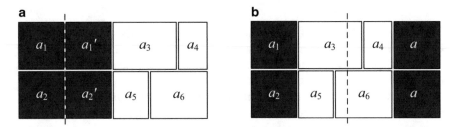

Fig. 3.2 Two symmetric-placement examples of a symmetry group $S_1 = \{(b_1, b'_1), (b_2, b'_2)\}$. **a** S_1 forms a symmetry island. **b** S_1 cannot form a symmetry island

2. *Symmetry Island*: This is a stricter restriction that can be put on symmetry groups. It was shown in [42] that the larger the distance between symmetric devices, the greater the difference between their electrical properties resulting in performance hindering phenomena. As such, a symmetry island is defined by a group of connected components that share a symmetry axis and should be placed in close proximity in order to reduce mismatch. An example is shown in Fig. 3.2.

3. *Common Centroid*: In order to minimize any stress-induced mismatch of the layout, the devices are decomposed into a set of equal device units and are arranged such that the centroid of the decomposed devices are located along the symmetry axis of both devices [42]. Figure 3.3 shows an example of two such common centroid layouts.

4. *Proximity*: A proximity constraint for a set of devices restricts the distance between the affected devices during placement. This constraint can help to reduce interconnecting wirelength, improve matching among devices. One common application of proximity constraints is when considering a hierarchical approach to layout design [44].

5. *Regularity*: According to [45], the arrangement of the layout structures in all levels (device level, cell level and block level) using the regular shapes shown in Fig. 3.4 results in a more compact layout, better routability and less sensitivity to process variation.

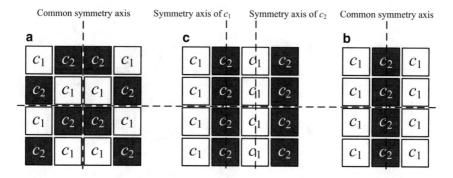

Fig. 3.3 Example of successful common centroid layouts: (**a**) and (**c**), And an unsuccessful example in (**b**)

Fig. 3.4 Regular shapes of placement

6. *Boundary*: The boundary constraint restricts an in-out device to the boundary of a rectangular area around its device group as shown in Fig. 3.5. This results in a reduced critical net wire length between the group and its external connections, leading to less parasitic and better performance [46].

7. *Current/Signal Flow*: As the most critical current/signal paths of an analog circuit usually have great impact on circuit performance, the devices in the same current/signal path should be placed in an order that minimizes the wirelength of the current/signal paths. As such, current paths should be designed monotonically [10] as shown in Fig. 3.6.

8. *Thermal*: If not taken into account, the improper placement of power devices close to thermally-sensitive devices might considerably reduce the circuit's performance. As such, thermal radiating devices should be placed taking into account a thermal symmetry axis in order to reduce any thermal gradients on the chip and reduce any mismatch across devices [43].

These constraints make the placement task a complicated one due to the numerous amount of inter-device relationships to be taken into account. In general, existing automatic placement generation solutions split into whether these constraints are handled explicitly or implicitly, explicit approaches mathematically describe the constraints in order to fulfill them while implicit approaches do not, and instead, the goal is generally to copy a valid placement that fulfills the constraints. Therefore, implicit approaches end up fulfilling the same constraints because by copying a

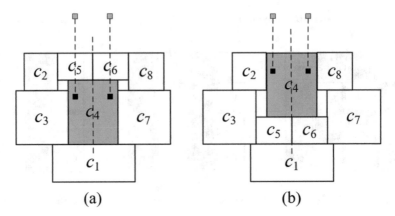

Fig. 3.5 Two symmetric placements of the op-amp. The module with input ports is placed **a** inside the symmetry island **b** on the top boundary of the symmetry island

valid placement, where valid implies constraint fulfillment, the produced placement is guaranteed to fulfill them. In this book, an explicit approach to the problem is studied with the intention of producing a versatile model capable of recognizing and meet these restrictions.

3.2   Placement Representation

In the literature, the many tools that attempt to automate placement generation can be distinguished by the representation of the cells, i.e. by how they encode and move the cells: absolute coordinates or topological representation.

- *Absolute Coordinates*: In the absolute representation, the optimizer moves the cells explicitly as each cell is represented by its absolute coordinates in an $\mathbb{R}^2$ coordinate system as done in [49]. Using this representation for the cells that make up the circuit, the previously defined constraints can easily be translated into an optimization problem in function of each cell's positioning, as such, this representation is recurrently used as a practical solution to layout constraint implementation. However, the lack of any restriction on the positioning of each cell allows the creation of invalid layouts with overlap between devices or unfulfilled symmetry constrains, as such, the search space includes both feasible and unfeasible solutions. Some approaches like [50] rely on a post-processing phase that converts the proposed solutions from absolute placement to a relative one where a deterministic cell slide technique is used in order to ensure a valid solution.
- *Relative Representation*: In the relative representation, the placement problem is encoded as a representative structure that details a set of constraints placed on the circuit [52] (visualized in Fig. 3.7) [53], e.g. device 1 is to the right of device 2.

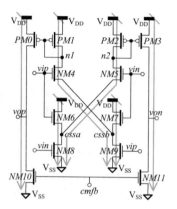

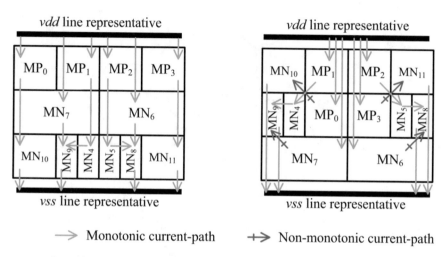

Fig. 3.6 a A placement with the consideration of the current flow constraints. **b** A placement without the consideration the current flow constraints. In blue: Monotonic current paths. In red: Non-monotonic current paths [47]

Thus the tool does not move the cells explicitly, instead, it changes the relative positions of cells by perturbing the representing structure. Due to this difference in representation, the search space is greatly reduced as it only contains admissible placements, however, it is not guaranteed that the optimal solution is included in it. Finally, a packing procedure must be performed to transform the relative representation into a floorplan while avoiding overlaps.

While it may seem that an absolute representation of the placement is more inefficient due to the inclusion of unfeasible solutions in the search space, recent efforts on stochastic/evolutionary algorithms suggest that searching the extensive search space associated to the use of absolute coordinates can compete with a search in the reduced solution space especially when taking into account the necessity for packing

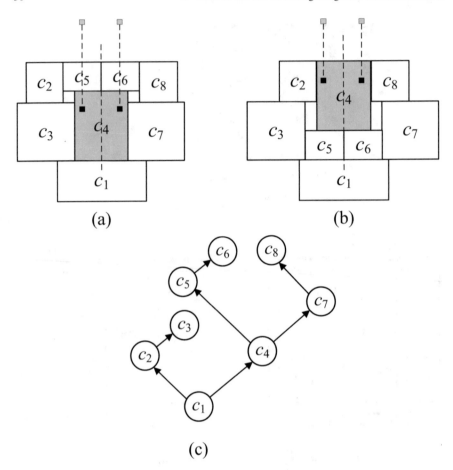

Fig. 3.7 a An admissable placement. **b** Its B*-tree representation. The binary tree is built in such a way that the relation between any two nodes contains information about their relative positioning in the produced layout, e.g. If node n_j is the left child of node n_i, module b_j must be located on the right-hand side and adjacent to module b_i

or structural scan techniques as post-processing tools in the topological representation framework [49]. Additionally, an absolute representation of the placement forms a very intuitive and general definition of the problem making further development and constraint handling easier.

3.3   Automatic Layout Generation Approaches

In order to increase the amount of automation in the process of analog layout synthesis, many new methodologies have been recently introduced. These can be divided

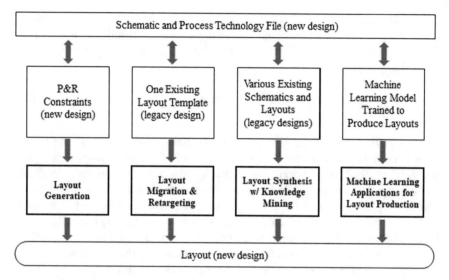

Fig. 3.8 Design flow of the major analog layout synthesis methodologies, distinguished by the number of previously existing solutions used during the process

into four main categories based on the number of legacy layouts used as reference when generating the solution for a given circuit. A legacy layout is defined as a previously developed layout solution that has been proven to have robust performance and fulfill the circuit's constraints. These previously developed solutions were the result of careful consideration and a long process of verification, as such, they embed in them the knowledge and effort of their designer. Some methodologies use these legacy layouts as a guideline for the development of the current layout in an attempt to recycle the work put into them. These approaches ultimately differ in whether or not the topological constraints of the circuit are handled explicitly.

The four main categories are the following:

- Placement Optimization Considering Topological Constrains
- Layout Migration and Retargeting
- Layout Synthesis through Knowledge Mining
- Machine Learning Applications towards Layout Production

Figure 3.8 represents the high level differences between the existing approaches.

3.3.1 Placement Optimization Considering Topological Constrains

This approach doesn't make use of any previous templates, instead, the topological constraints mentioned in Sect. 3.1 are codified in a cost function dependent on the devices' positioning and are dealt with explicitly. In the absolute coordinate's framework, the circuit's constraints can be translated and quantified through a cost function. Take an example from [54] where the cost function to be minimized is defined as

$$f(x) = \alpha_1 f_1(x) + \alpha_2 f_2(x) + \sum_i \alpha_i f_i(x), \tag{3.1}$$

where x is the design variables vector (i.e. coordinates and, if allowed, the rotation of each cell) and α is the weight's vector for each of the cost components; $f_1(x)$ and $f_2(x)$ are the two fundamental objectives to be achieved/minimized, circuit area and overlap. The remaining $f_i(x)$ represent any remaining objectives. As such, the absolute representation of the problem allows a simple mapping between device placement and restriction satisfaction. For example, in [54], $f_2(x)$ is forcibly driven to 0, that is, no overlap is allowed in the final solutions. Once the problem is defined as a cost function, optimization framework can be used to find a solution.

Using a relative description of a placement, these constraints can be enforced through either the penalization of unfeasible solutions, the avoidance of these solutions altogether (through a representation that directly enforces the fulfillment of these constraints) or through post-processing fixes. In [51], each placement proposed by a B*-tree is evaluated for the fulfillment of symmetry constraints and corrections are made such that these constraints are directly taken into account during the exploration of the solution space. Still, symmetry is the only out of the eight constraints mentioned in Sect. 3.1 that is enforced in the solution. In matter of fact, this methodology requires a very thorough definition of the problem in order to ensure a meaningful solution, i.e. it is needed to make explicit all the constraints that should be taken into account, which might differ on a problem basis, when designing the solution, or else the results might be quite unexpected.

3.3.2   Layout Migration and Retargeting

This methodology makes use of the fact that the circuit currently being designed has been designed before, thus the existence of a proven quality layout for the considered topology is assured. As such, the legacy layout can be used as a guideline for device placement in order to fulfill the design constraints. These approaches start by extracting from the existing layout the relative positioning of the devices that serves as the layout's representation and as the guideline for the new layout [55, 56].

These solutions enable the conservation and re-utilization of the knowledge and careful considerations put into the design of the tested legacy layout. However, in some cases, the new dimensions of the circuit being designed prevent the direct use of the legacy layout's relative placement, the difference in size of the devices may either make the layout invalid due to unmet constraints or enable further optimization of some metrics like chip area; and, when using a different process technology imposes some design rules that must now be taken into account making the proposed solutions seldom optimal. In an effort to address these issues, some approaches try to combine the use of legacy information with layout generation approaches [48].

3.3.3 Layout Synthesis Through Knowledge Mining

The methodology described in the previous section requires the existence of a legacy layout of the exact same circuit, which constitutes a limitation to the design of circuits without previously qualified layouts and doesn't make use of the immense knowledge database that all of the legacy layouts constitute in the scenario of existing matching sub-circuits. To address these limitations, some new solutions based in knowledge mining were proposed in [57, 58].

In these approaches the solution is based on several examples taken from a design repository composed by quality-approved layouts for many different circuit topologies. The process consists in first matching sub-circuits from the input circuit to the sub-circuits extracted from any of the layouts in the repository, note that the same sub-circuit can have more than one match in the repository allowing the generation of several possible layouts for each combination of sub-circuits matched. In [57], each layout in the repository is translated into a connected graph that encodes the nature of the connections between its composing devices, with the same being done to the circuit being currently designed. Once the circuits are translated into graphs the problem to identify all common sub-circuits that have the same device types, device constraints, and interconnections between the two layouts becomes a problem of graph matching (i.e. graph isomorphism, sub-graph isomorphism or sub-graph identification [59])

This methodology allows the mixture of the spread-out knowledge in the repository. However, as the dataset increases the comparison with every layout can prove computationally demanding, additionally conflicts are deterministically solved, as the acquired knowledge is not generalized but only applied being impossible to generate a layout beyond training data.

3.3.4 Machine Learning Applications Towards Layout Production

A recent approach following the Knowledge Mining methodology makes use of artificial neural networks (ANNs) in order to develop an automatic placement model that generates for a given circuit topology using different previously produced legacy layouts, new placements at push-button speed [12]. In [12], the dataset consisted in several combinations of dimensions for each of the 12 devices that form the single stage amplifier (SSA) circuit from [60] that can be visualized in Fig. 3.9.

Table 3.1 Device sizing info dataset used as input in [12]

Example #	Device 0					...	Device 11				
	w_0	l_0	nf_0	dw_0	dh_0	...	w_11	l_11	nf_11	dw_0	dh_0
	(μm)	(μm)		(μm)	(μm)		(μm)	(μm)		(μm)	(μm)
0	17.5	0.36	3	3.48	8.07	...	8.7	0.89	3	4.73	5.14
1	17.7	0.36	7	6.52	4.765	...	83.3	0.83	7	9.47	14.4
...	...	...	...	...	...	...	...	...	...	...	...

For each device of the circuit, 5 sizing variables were stored in each example, the channel's width, the channel's length, the number of fingers and the encapsulated module's width and height (the device's effective width and height in the layout). So, each example in the dataset consists in a specific combination of values for each of the devices' sizing characteristics (a sizing scenario), these were the features used for the model. An example of the device sizing data is shown in Table 3.1. This input vector is denominated *5-sizing*.

The solution was designed with the intention of generalizing the designers' knowledge through the inclusion of a target for each of these examples. For each example, 12 template based placements were built using current computer aided design (CAD)

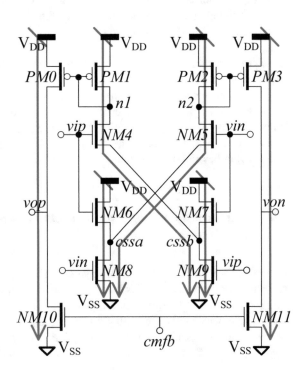

Fig. 3.9 Single stage amplifier with gain enhancement: schematic with current paths highlighted [47]

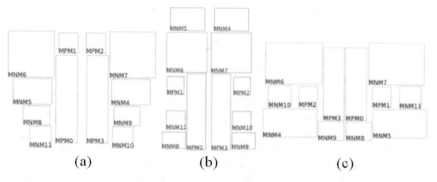

Fig. 3.10 Three different templates for the SSA circuit, each described by the relative positioning of each device

Table 3.2 Device positioning per template

Example #	Template 0						...	Template 11					
	area_0	x_0	y_0	...	x_11	y_11	...	area_11	x_0	y_0	...	x_11	x_11
	(μm^2)	(μm)	(μm)		(μm)	(μm)		(μm)	(μm)	(μm)		(μm)	(μm)
0	2052.7	10.71	4.01	...	15.44	4.01	...	24.23	6.69	6.39	...	6.69	0.0
1	3529.8	18.49	4.01	...	26.26	4.01	...	33.57	6.69	15.39	...	6.69	0.0
...	...	...	...	...	...	...	...	...	...	...	...	...	...

tools. These templates serve as general guidelines to determine the relative positioning of each device, and are shared among all examples. They account for the slight adjustments required to accommodate the sizing differences between the examples. Figure 3.10 shows 3 of the 12 templates considered. Take the example of Fig. 3.10b, it can be described by the relative positioning of each device, MNM5 is to the left of MNM4 that is above MNM7, whereas the leftmost template can be described by device MNM7 being above MNM4 and so on.

The process for generating these templates makes use of the layout migration tools previously explained, once the relative positioning description of each template is properly formulated, through layout migration techniques, it is possible to apply them to every sizing case in the dataset.

As such, for each example in the dataset, each device's absolute positioning in each of the 12 generated placements is stored as shown in Table 3.2. For each of the examples only one of the generated placements is used as target, the one with minimum area (in [12] the network is trained to generate three predictions, one with the smallest area, the smallest width and smallest height, however, for simplification purposes, here we consider only the smallest area output since the process is identical for the three cases changing only the criterion used for template selection).

Once each sizing scenario has been assigned a placement as target, the model's learning process consists in approximating its predictions to the assigned target through the mean squared error (MSE) loss function defined through

$$MSE = \frac{1}{n} \sum_{i=1}^{n} (Y_i - \hat{Y}_i)^2. \tag{3.2}$$

where Y is the prediction vector with x, y coordinates for each of the 12 devices, similarly $\hat{Y}$ contains the x, y target coordinates for each device. These targets are the human knowledge fed into the system.

Building a model that minimizes the MSE function results in the minimum average difference between the predictions made and the given knowledge. In other words, a model trained to minimize this function results in a map from the feature space to the label space in such a way that minimizes the difference between the predictions made and the given labels. The labels act as a guideline to the model's behavior and is expected that this relation, fed to the model in the shape of *features, labels* pairs, is extrapolated to the rest of the feature space.

By selecting only 1 of the 12 templates as target for each of the examples, the model is punished (through a high loss) for following one of the remaining templates instead. As such, the model is not encouraged to innovate and, for example, mix the existing templates, as this behavior results in higher MSE error, which the model is trained to minimize. This work builds on top of this model, and, to address this issue, a new loss function is designed, one that encourages the exploration of a multitude of different relative device positioning.

3.4   Conclusions

In this chapter, the current approaches towards automatic layout generation were categorized depending on the number of considered pre-existent guidelines. Approaches that consider legacy layouts do not produce novel predictions, instead, pre-existing knowledge is reused and nothing is gained knowledge wise. On the other hand, approaches that rely on the optimization of certain quality metrics are generally time-consuming and computationally heavy.

A novel approach, introduced in [12], implemented ANNs in order to make the process of template selection and migration in practice instantaneous. However, similarly to Knowledge Mining and Layout Migration (in between of which the approach might be placed), this approach does not promote innovation or knowledge generalization and might even punish the behavior. This makes the model behave similarly to classification models, assigning to each example a class in the form of positioning guidelines (template). Additionally, the process of template pre-production might present a challenge in itself, consequently if no template was produced for a given topology, the model would just use another topology's template as target, producing an invalid placement. However this approach reveals the capabilities of the ANNs as an alternative for automatic push-button analog IC placement. Table 3.3 summarizes the relevant comparisons between the four different discussed methodologies.

Table 3.3 Comparison table for automatic placement methodologies. $(+/-)$ indicates advantages/disadvantages

	Multi Topology Support	Solution Optimality	Computational Effort	Knowledge Generalization	Dependency of Legacy Data
Placement Optimization	Allows any circuit to be optimized from a set of topological constraints (-) Describing an exhaustive set of constraints for a meaningful circuit optimization process can be challenging	Locally or Globally quasi-optimal (+) The solution is designed specifically for the topology and set of devices sizes'	(-) Global optimality is time consuming (-) As each solution is generated independently, a large solution space must be explored	As solutions are created independently, no knowledge is transferred from one solution to the other	No past solutions are necessary
Layout Migration	Migrates placements for a given circuit topology (-) Limited to previously designed circuits	(-) Optimality is not ensured	(+) Relative fast generation times, as most of it is consumed in validation procedures	(+) The knowledge of an expert designer is directly reused in a new scenario	Requires one valid solution for the circuit
Knowledge Mining	Limited to circuits whose composing parts are common to previously designed circuits	(-) Optimality is not ensured Approach is more tailored for the different topologies than simple layout migration	(-) Searching for matching blocks through a vast library is time consuming (-) Upper level block incompatibilities and conflicts might result in costly backtracking	(+) The knowledge of various expert designers is reused in each new generation	A solution is not guaranteed if it cannot be built from the blocks available from previous solutions Several previous solutions are necessary to ensure that a new solution can be built
Machine Learning	(-) Models are built for single topology use The considered scope is directly related to the model's complexity	(-) Optimality is not ensured, however, if the model is capable of properly abstracting the acquired knowledge, solutions' quality is improved	(-) Model training can be time consuming (+) Single solution is produced at push-button speed	(+) The knowledge of various expert designers is abstracted A solution is built using the observed pattern guidelines	To ensure good generalization capabilities, many previous solutions should be compiled Solution variability promotes abstraction and increases generalization
This Work	(+) Capable of dealing with circuits with up to a certain number of devices with topological constraints	(+) The use of an optimization based loss function improves optimality compared to previous machine learning approaches (+) More explicit definition of the goals makes the model more likely to abstract them	(-) Model training can be time consuming (+) Batch solutions are produced at push-button speed	During training, the model learns from its attempts and extrapolates them to the complete design space (+) A solution is designed considering the results from many previous training scenarios	No past layout solutions are necessary

In this work, the use of ANNs is further explored, in an attempt to use its fast, generalizing predictive prowess to produce optimized, topological constraint aware placements inspired by the Placement Optimization approach, while minimizing the time cost usually associated with it.

This work takes a somewhat Supervised approach to the problem since there is a target for the network, to predict placements that fulfill all of the circuit's topological constraints. However, this target is somewhat unclear as there is no single correct answer, instead, a multitude of predictions are allowed, as long as they fulfill the topological constraints of the circuit. This process could be converted to a classic Supervised Learning approach if, for every example in the dataset, all the placements that fulfill the circuit's topological constraints were generated and the error associated to a specific example's prediction would be given by the minimum, for example, MSE error across all the generated target placements. In a way, the developed loss function describes abstractly all these possible placements and directs the model to the closest one.

Chapter 4
ANN Models for Analog Placement Automation

In this chapter, several artificial neural network (ANN) models towards analog place-ment automation are thoroughly analyzed and compared starting with the model from [12]. This comparison is made in order to properly identify their strengths and weak-nesses, and, develop a model that combines their strong points addressing their weak points.

4.1 Problem Definition and Feature Description

The dataset used in [12] consisted in several sizing examples of the same circuit topology. Each sizing scenario was represented by a *5-sizing* input vector similar to each row in Table 4.1. For each sizing scenario 12 templates were designed out of which one was used as target placement (the one with smallest area). The ANN model's predictions were evaluated by comparing them to these selected targets, if the predictions made were very similar, the error would be low.

While in [12] the scope of the solution consisted only of ANN models that produce different layouts for a single circuit topology (the single stage amplifier (SSA) from [60]), the solution here developed intends to expand the scope of the ANN, making it able to design placements for multiple circuit topologies, as such, a new circuit is introduced in the training data as well as a testing circuit (not included in the training data) in order to evaluate the model's performance to topologies never seen before. The purpose of introducing this new circuit in the training data is to not only subject the model to new patterns of topological constraints but as well to test the model's capability of dealing with topologies with different number of devices.

The additional training circuit, the cascode free single stage amplifier (CFSSA), was presented in [61] and its schematic can be seen in Fig. 4.1b.

However, the introduction of these new circuits brings some issues. The number of devices is different, which would make the input vector's length different for each case. Also, even if the number of devices is not different, if the circuit topology is

© The Author(s), under exclusive license to Springer Nature Switzerland AG 2020

A. Gusmão et al., *Analog IC Placement Generation via Neural Networks from Unlabeled Data*, SpringerBriefs in Applied Sciences and Technology, https://doi.org/10.1007/978-3-030-50061-0_4

Table 4.1 Device sizing info dataset used as input in [12]

Example #	Device 0					...	Device 11				
	w_0	l_0	nf_0	dw_0	dh_0	...	w_11	l_11	nf_11	dw_0	dh_0
	(μm)	(μm)		(μm)	(μm)		(μm)	(μm)		(μm)	(μm)
0	17.5	0.36	3	3.48	8.07	...	8.7	0.89	3	4.73	5.14
1	17.7	0.36	7	6.52	4.765	...	83.3	0.83	7	9.47	14.4
...	...	...	...	...	...	...	...	...	...	...	...

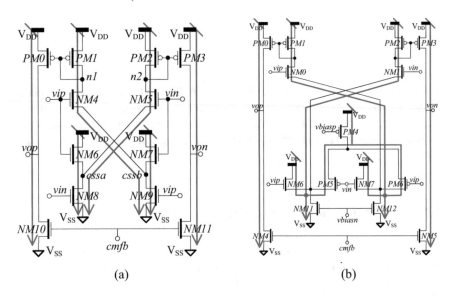

(a)   (b)

Fig. 4.1 Training dataset's circuit topologies: **a** Single stage amplifier with gain enhancement: schematic with current paths highlighted. **b** Cascode Free Single Stage Amplifier: schematic with current paths highlighted [3]

different, how would the ANN distinguish between examples? It is not far fetched to think of another circuit with 12 devices with similar sizing characteristics but very different topology, that is, very different symmetry or current flow constraints (that were explained in Chap. 3), if so, the templates used for the SSA would most likely be invalid for this new topology. Using only the sizing of the devices to identify the circuit topology is not enough as the same combination of features would have different expected outputs.

4.2   Constraint Descriptive Vector

A new feature vector is here proposed that addresses both the issue of input examples collision (two different topologies with a different expected prediction having the same input vector) and promote more diverse and tailor made solutions for each example. The objective is to build a model capable of interpreting the topological constraints of the circuit given as input and producing an optimal, and valid (that fulfills all constraints it is subject to) placement.

Two topological constraints are considered in the design of this solution, current flow (or monotonic current path) and symmetry. In order to enable the ANN to interpret these constraints, they should be somehow encoded in the input vector, as such, the new input vector now includes not only each devices' sizing characteristics but also a description of each devices' symmetry and current flow constraints. These constraints are described as existing relations between every pair of devices. This device level description of the problem should contribute to the model's generalization capabilities since every new problem (newly introduced topology never seen before) can be decomposed into smaller sub-problems that can then possibly be matched to similar sub-problems that follow patterns from the training set, possibly reducing the level of extrapolation necessary to produce a layout.

4.2.1   Current Flow Encoding

Current flow constraints describe the path the current takes (through which devices it passes in order) from the power source to the ground. The devices should be placed in such an order that the current flows monotonically in one direction [10].

In the case of the SSA in Fig. 4.1a, it is possible to distinguish six different current paths. As aforementioned, these paths can be described by the list of devices through which the current passes in order, that is, as if one were to trace a path from the power source to the ground and registering through which devices it would pass. For example, one valid description of a current path would be *[PM0, NM10]* as well as *[PM1, NM4, NM9]* and *[NM7, NM9]*. To describe these different paths locally from the view of each individual device, it is sufficient to keep track from which device(s) the current has flowed from and towards which device(s) the current flows towards. As such, for each of the 12 devices that constitute the circuit, it is necessary to describe its positioning relative to every other in the layout. So for each device, its current flow constraints can be represented by the vector of length equal to the number of devices in the topology (12 in this case), where each entry indicates whether the considered device either immediately succeeds or precedes any of the other devices in the topology on some current path.

For example, the device *NM9* is contained in two different current paths, in both as the last device in the path, succeeding device *NM4* and *NM7*. Therefore, its current flow constraint descriptive vector is defined as $[0, 0, 0, 0, -1, 0, 0, -1, 0, 0, 0, 0]$

Table 4.2 SSA circuit device's current flow constraints description vector

	PM0	PM1	PM2	PM3	NM4	NM5	NM6	NM7	NM8	NM9	NM10	NM11
PM0	0	0	0	0	0	0	0	0	0	0	1	0
PM1	0	0	0	0	1	0	0	0	0	0	0	0
PM2	0	0	0	0	0	1	0	0	0	0	0	0
PM3	0	0	0	0	0	0	0	0	0	0	0	1
NM4	0	-1	0	0	0	0	0	0	0	1	0	0
NM5	0	0	-1	0	0	0	0	0	1	0	0	0
NM6	0	0	0	0	0	0	0	0	1	0	0	0
NM7	0	0	0	0	0	0	0	0	0	1	0	0
NM8	0	0	0	0	0	-1	-1	0	0	0	0	0
NM9	0	0	0	0	-1	0	0	-1	0	0	0	0
NM10	-1	0	0	0	0	0	0	0	0	0	0	0
NM11	0	0	0	-1	0	0	0	0	0	0	0	0

where each entry of the vector encodes *NM9*'s relation to any of the devices in the circuit. The order in which the devices appear in is completely arbitrary and will be discussed thoroughly in Sect. 4.2.5. For this example, assume the order represented in Table 4.2. Assuming this order, in the vector the -1 appears in positions 5 and 8 (that represent device *NM4* and *NM7* respectively), indicating that these appear immediately before device $NM9$ in any given current path of the considered topology. Analogously, for device *NM4*, its current flow constraint descriptive vector is defined as $[0, -1, 0, 0, 0, 0, 0, 0, 0, 1, 0, 0]$, meaning the device succeeds device *PM1* and precedes *NM9* in a path (might not be the same path, but that is unnecessary information for the task at hand). The full current flow constraints descriptive vector for each of the 12 devices in the SSA topology is shown in Table 4.2.

Using the same method, Table 4.3 shows the full current flow constraints descriptive vector for each of the devices that constitute the CFSSA.

The length of this vector, for each device, is thus given by:

$$L_{cf} = N, \tag{4.1}$$

where N represents the number of composing devices for any given circuit topology. So, for each of the two circuit topologies contained in the training dataset, the length of the current flow constraint description vector for each device is given by:

$$L_{cf}(SSA) = 12; \tag{4.2}$$
$$L_{cf}(CFSSA) = 15. \tag{4.3}$$

Table 4.3 CFSSA circuit device's current flow description

	PM0	PM1	PM2	PM3	NM0	NM1	PM4	NM6	PM5	NM7	PM6	NM8	NM9	NM4	NM5
PM0	0	0	0	0	0	0	0	0	0	0	0	0	0	1	0
PM1	0	0	0	0	1	0	0	0	0	0	0	0	0	0	0
PM2	0	0	0	0	0	1	0	0	0	0	0	0	0	0	0
PM3	0	0	0	0	0	0	0	0	0	0	0	0	0	0	1
NM0	0	-1	0	0	0	0	0	0	0	0	0	0	1	0	0
NM1	0	0	-1	0	0	0	0	0	0	0	0	1	0	0	0
PM4	0	0	0	0	0	0	0	0	1	0	1	0	0	0	0
NM6	0	0	0	0	0	0	0	0	0	0	0	1	0	0	0
PM5	0	0	0	0	0	0	-1	0	0	0	0	1	0	0	0
NM7	0	0	0	0	0	0	0	0	0	0	0	0	1	0	0
PM6	0	0	0	0	0	0	-1	0	0	0	0	1	0	0	0
NM8	0	0	0	0	0	0	-1	-1	-1	0	0	0	0	0	0
NM9	0	0	0	0	0	0	-1	0	0	-1	-1	0	0	0	0
NM4	-1	0	0	0	0	0	0	0	0	0	0	0	0	0	0
NM5	0	0	0	-1	0	0	0	0	0	0	0	0	0	0	0

4.2.2 Symmetry

A symmetry constraint corresponds to a set of devices and/or device pairs that are symmetrically placed along a symmetry axis.

In the case of the SSA, each of the devices has a symmetric pair, as is the case of the pair of devices *[PM0, PM3]* and *[NM6, NM7]*. Once again, these constraints can be encoded through the use of a one-hot vector for each of the devices that indicates to which of the circuit's N devices it should be symmetric to. As such, the result is, for each device, an $N = 12$ long vector, e.g. for device *PM0*: [0, 0, 0, 1, 0, 0, 0, 0, 0, 0, 0, 0], or for device *NM6*: [0, 0, 0, 0, 0, 0, 0, 1, 0, 0, 0, 0]. The full symmetry constraints descriptive vectors for the devices of the SSA are shown in the rows of Table 4.4, for the CFSSA in Table 4.5.

Table 4.4 SSA circuit device's symmetry description

	PM0	PM1	PM2	PM3	NM4	NM5	NM6	NM7	NM8	NM9	NM10	NM11
PM0	0	0	0	1	0	0	0	0	0	0	0	0
PM1	0	0	1	0	0	0	0	0	0	0	0	0
PM2	0	1	0	0	0	0	0	0	0	0	0	0
PM3	1	0	0	0	0	0	0	0	0	0	0	0
NM4	0	0	0	0	0	1	0	0	0	0	0	0
NM5	0	0	0	0	1	0	0	0	0	0	0	0
NM6	0	0	0	0	0	0	0	1	0	0	0	0
NM7	0	0	0	0	0	0	1	0	0	0	0	0
NM8	0	0	0	0	0	0	0	0	0	1	0	0
NM9	0	0	0	0	0	0	0	0	1	0	0	0
NM10	0	0	0	0	0	0	0	0	0	0	0	1
NM11	0	0	0	0	0	0	0	0	0	0	1	0

Table 4.5 CFSSA circuit device's symmetry description

	PM0	PM1	PM2	PM3	NM0	NM1	PM4	NM6	PM5	NM7	PM6	NM8	NM9	NM4	NM5
PM0	0	0	0	1	0	0	0	0	0	0	0	0	0	0	0
PM1	0	0	1	0	0	0	0	0	0	0	0	0	0	0	0
PM2	0	1	0	0	0	0	0	0	0	0	0	0	0	0	0
PM3	1	0	0	0	0	0	0	0	0	0	0	0	0	0	0
NM0	0	0	0	0	0	1	0	0	0	0	0	0	0	0	0
NM1	0	0	0	0	1	0	0	0	0	0	0	0	0	0	0
PM4	0	0	0	0	0	0	1	0	0	0	0	0	0	0	0
NM6	0	0	0	0	0	0	0	0	0	0	1	0	0	0	0
PM5	0	0	0	0	0	0	0	0	0	1	0	0	0	0	0
NM7	0	0	0	0	0	0	0	0	1	0	0	0	0	0	0
PM6	0	0	0	0	0	0	0	1	0	0	0	0	0	0	0
NM8	0	0	0	0	0	0	0	0	0	0	0	0	1	0	0
NM9	0	0	0	0	0	0	0	0	0	0	0	1	0	0	0
NM4	0	0	0	0	0	0	0	0	0	0	0	0	0	0	1
NM5	0	0	0	0	0	0	0	0	0	0	0	0	0	1	0

Note from Table 4.5 that this representation can also encode self-symmetric devices (devices that should be centered along the symmetry axis) as is the case of for example device *PM4* from the CFSSA, these devices' constraints can be encoded through a 1 in their own index. Devices that are not constrained whatsoever (i.e. autonomous cells) would be encoded by having no 1 along their vector.

The symmetry constraint descriptive vector's length for each device is given by:

$$L_{sym} = N, \tag{4.4}$$

where N represents the number of composing devices for any given circuit topology. So for the two circuit topologies used:

$$L_{sym}(SSA) = 12; \tag{4.5}$$
$$L_{sym}(CFSSA) = 15. \tag{4.6}$$

4.2.3   Sizing

Since now the introduction of both the current flow and symmetry constraints serve as distinguishing factors between two different circuit topologies, the only sizing characteristics of each device that directly influence the placement task are its encapsulation's width and height. As such, these are the only two sizing characteristics out of the five shown in Table 4.1 that are used in the constraint description vector. So, for each device, a two values long vector is kept *[width, height]*.

Table 4.6 SSA circuit device's sizing description and normalization

Example #	Non Normalized					Normalized				
	PM0		...	NM11		PM0		...	NM11	
	w[μ m]	h[μ m]	...	w[μ m]	h[μ m]	w	h	...	w	h
0	3.48	8.07	...	4.73	5.14	-0.55	0.32	...	-0.12	-0.15
1	6.52	4.76	...	9.47	14.4	0.47	-0.21	...	1.47	1.40
...	...	...	...	...	...	...	...	...	...	...
μ	5.11	6.06	...	5.08	6.03	0	0	...	0	0
σ	2.99	6.20	...	2.98	5.98	1	1	...	1	1

As explained in Sect. 2.8, quantifiable features should be scaled in order to avoid overfitting. In this case, the fact that the features refer to devices' sizes on nanometric integration technologies, it is important that these values are scaled in order to avoid any vanishing gradients during the backpropagation phase. Therefore, the sizing characteristics of each device are normalized using:

$$x' = \frac{x - \mu}{\sigma} \tag{4.7}$$

(detailed in Chap. 2 of this book) across all examples as shown in Table 4.6.

4.2.4 Zero Padding for Multiple Circuit Design

By aggregating these three components of a device's description into one vector the result is a vector per device of length:

$$L_{dev} = 2N + 2. \tag{4.8}$$

In the case of the SSA, the vector's length is given by $2 \times 12 + 2 = 26$. An example of a full, scaled, device descriptive vector for device *PM0* in a sizing scenario of the SSA is given in Fig. 4.2.

For devices of the CFSSA circuit topologies, through Eqs. 4.1 and 4.4, their descriptive vector's length is given by:

$$L_{dev}(CFSSA) = 2 \times 15 + 2 = 32 \tag{4.9}$$

Finally, the complete input vector of a sizing case for the SSA and the CFSSA circuits are the result of the concatenation of the descriptive vectors of all composing N devices as shown in Fig. 4.3.

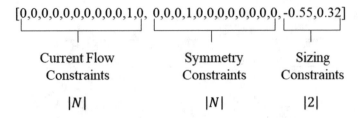

$$[0,0,0,0,0,0,0,0,0,1,0, \; 0,0,0,1,0,0,0,0,0,0,0,0, \; -0.55,0.32]$$

Current Flow	Symmetry	Sizing
Constraints	Constraints	Constraints
$|N|$	$|N|$	$|2|$

Fig. 4.2 Example of the scaled, descriptive vector of the device *PM0* in the single stage amplifier circuit

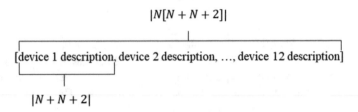

$$|N[N+N+2]|$$

[device 1 description, device 2 description, ..., device 12 description]

$$|N+N+2|$$

Fig. 4.3 Structure of the input vector for the SSA topology

Considering the concatenation of N constraint descriptive vectors, the length of a circuit's input vector is given by:

$$L = N[2N + 2], \tag{4.10}$$

So, replacing by the values of each circuit topology, its specific input vector length is given by:

$$L(SSA) = 12[2 \times 12 + 2] = 312 \tag{4.11}$$

$$L(CFSSA) = 15[2 \times 15 + 2] = 480 \tag{4.12}$$

Recall from Chap. 2 of this book that an ANN's number of nodes in the input layer is usually the number of features considered, that is, the size of the input vector. Note also that the input vector's length depends on the input circuit's topology and since an ANN's structure is not changeable depending on the input, a general input vector length must be defined. This is necessary because it is the objective of this work to build a network capable of formulating placements for different circuit topologies, otherwise, three different networks with different structures would be more effective for each individual circuit. Naturally, smaller input vectors will be padded with zeros to match the largest input vector's length, since the length of the topology's input vector only depends on the number of considered devices, it is sufficient to define a maximum number of devices to be considered by the model. Since in this scenario, only 2 topologies are considered, the maximum number of devices allowed is given by the maximum number of devices across both topologies, which is the CFSSA's

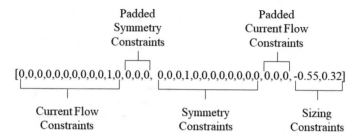

Fig. 4.4 Example of the scaled padded descriptive vector of the device *PM0* in the single stage amplifier circuit

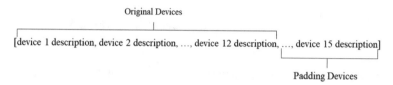

Fig. 4.5 Structure of the padded input vector for the SSA topology

15. As such 3 devices with no current flow or symmetry constraints, as well as no sizing characteristics, are added to the SSA topology.

Therefore, the current flow vectors of the SSA devices are padded with two empty devices, i.e. devices that no current flows into or from. For the symmetry constraint descriptive vector, it is only necessary to add autonomous cells (devices with no symmetry constraints) in order to match the 15 devices from the CFSSA. The new padded descriptive vector of the device *PM0* in the SSA circuit can be seen in Fig. 4.4.

Finally, the resulting padded input vector's length is given by:

$$length = \max_{t_i}(N(t_i))[2\max_{t_i}(N(t_i)) + 2], \qquad (4.13)$$

where $N(t_i)$ denotes the number of devices in topology i. The final shape of a padded input vector can be visualized in Fig. 4.5.

4.2.5   Device Scrambling

In order to avoid the model to learn from the order of the constraints in the input vector, for every example, the order of the devices is scrambled. In real life scenarios, the order of the devices through which a circuit is described is not fixed, so naturally, the network should be robust to a random ordering. Some pre-processing procedures could be implemented to ensure the order would be constant, however, these would most certainly have to be highly sophisticated in order to deal with inevitable ambiguity scenarios.

Fig. 4.6 Device scramble
transformation example

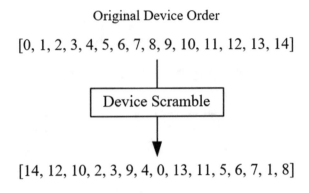

Fig. 4.6 Device scramble transformation example

Take the example of sorting the devices of the SSA circuit by following the current path from the power source to the ground. Six different devices, with very different properties are directly connected to the power source, so what is the criterion to distinguish between them and consistently select the same device to appear first? Additionally, assume such criterion is achievable, by introducing this pre-processing stage in the model, a new layer of variability is being introduced. In the given example of sorting devices by following the current path, the order of the devices would inevitably contain information regarding the current paths themselves, allowing the model to learn using the order of the devices as basis instead of the constraint description. This would be highly unstable since the pre-processing stage would be, from the model's point of view, a black box. So for maximum generalization, the model would have to learn to fully interpret the introduced pre-processing stage. By not including this stage, the model is being forced to interpret the constraints that were provided, promoting a more stable, robust and generalizing model. As such, the model is trained with the order of the devices independently scrambled for each example. Considering 15 devices, the number of possible permutations of a single example is $15! \sim 1.31 \times 10^{12}$. Figure 4.6 shows an example of scrambling the order of 15 devices.

To apply the effects of changing the order of devices at every level, it is necessary to consider its effects on the current flow and symmetry constraints descriptive vectors of each device. For the symmetry constraints, consider the CFSSA's symmetry Table 4.5. Changing the order of the rows is not enough and thus the order of the columns should be changed as well in succession. This corresponds to the transformation applied to each device's symmetry constraints vector. The exact same transformation is applied to the current flow constraint descriptive vectors. At the input vector level, it is only necessary to change the order through which one concatenates the devices' descriptive vectors as illustrated in Fig. 4.7.

[device 0 description, device 1 description,..., device 14 description]

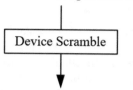

[device 14 description, device 12 description,..., device 8 description]

Fig. 4.7 Device scramble at input vector level

4.3 Topological Loss Function

In order to focus the model on learning how to interpret a circuit's topological constraints, it is necessary to change its loss function since, as aforementioned, the mean squared error (MSE) used in [12] evaluates the quality of the prediction made by comparing its similarities to the selected legacy layout. This results on the focus being in generating layouts similar to previously designed layouts, which in turn discourages the production of novel designs and creates a model unprepared for new circuit topologies. The use of the MSE loss function also demands the production of several previously tested legacy designs that may prove a challenge in itself. To overcome these issues, a new topological loss function (TLF) is proposed, one that evaluates the quality of a prediction made by evaluating whether or not the circuit's placement constraints are met. Therefore, the general shape of the proposed topological loss function is given by:

$$loss = w_a W_A + w_s S + w_{cf} C_F + w_o O, \tag{4.14}$$

where W_A denotes the wasted area of the layout, S represents the deviation from optimal symmetry, C_F represents the error associated to non-monotonic current flow directions, O denotes the summed overlap area between all devices and $w_{a,s,cf,o}$ represent the weights associated to the wasted area, symmetry, current flow and overlap errors respectively.

Similarly to the produced input vector that focused on describing the constraints of the full topology by decomposing them into inter-devices relations, the loss function evaluates the quality of a given placement as the mean existing error between device relations, making the error easily decomposed into more specific components that can be directly targeted.

4.3.1 Wasted Area and Overlap Between Devices

It is a usual requirement during the implementation of analog circuits in CMOS technologies to have minimal area in order to reduce costs, as such, the first factor taken into account in the new loss function is the layout's compactness.

In order to reduce as much as possible the layout's area, it is analogous to reduce the average minimum distance between all devices in the layout that corresponds to the implemented metric in the model. However, while it is desirable for devices to be pushed closer together in order to increase the placement's compactness, devices should not ever be placed on top of each other. As explained in Chap. 3 of this book, the use of absolute coordinates allows devices to occupy the same region in the 2D plane as exemplified in Fig. 4.8.

Naturally, for a final placement to be valid, no pair of devices should be overlapped and such occurrences should be taken into account by the designed loss function. These two errors, wasted area and overlap, are naturally contrary to each other, while one punishes distance between devices, the other punishes cases where the distance is too small (negative). This duality makes both components easy to encode in conjunction since both ultimately rely on measuring the minimum distance between pair of devices.

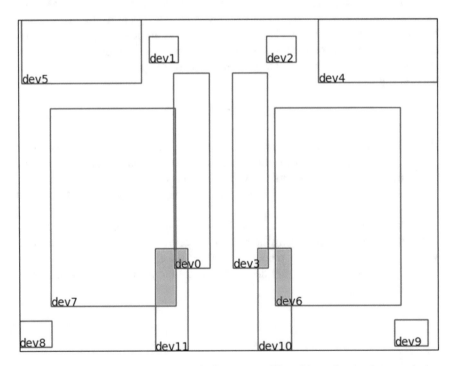

Fig. 4.8 Example of a placement for the single-stage amplifier with overlap area between devices in gray

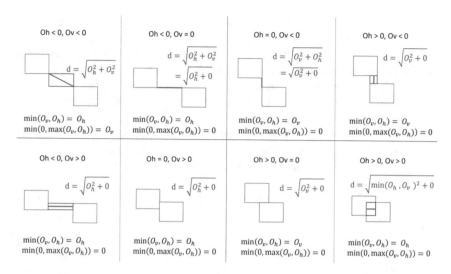

Fig. 4.9 Case study of proximity and overlap situations that can both be measured through the minimum distance between devices

The minimum possible distance between two rectangles in an $\mathbb{R}^2$ space can be calculated using the dimensions of the overlap rectangle between each pair of devices as shown in Fig. 4.9. The dimensions of the overlap rectangle are defined by the existing vertical and horizontal overlap. Vertical/horizontal overlap are defined as the overlap between the two lines that result from the projection of both rectangles in the vertical/horizontal axis and can be calculated through:

$$O_H(i, j) = max(0, min(x_i^+, x_j^+) - max(x_i^-, x_j^-)) \tag{4.15}$$

and:

$$O_V(i, j) = max(0, min(y_i^+, y_j^+) - max(y_i^-, y_j^-)), \tag{4.16}$$

where $x_i^{+/-}$ represents the right/left x coordinate of device i, and $y_i^{+/-}$ represents the top/bottom y coordinate of device i. Note that the sign of the vertical/horizontal overlap indicates whether or not the devices' vertical/horizontal projections are overlapped.

Note from Fig. 4.9 that overlap only occurs when both these components are positive (indicating that there is overlap in both projections). The minimum distance between any two rectangles using the considered overlap components can seamlessly be calculated through:

$$d(i, j) = \sqrt{min(O_v(i, j), O_h(i, j))^2 + min(0, max(O_v(i, j), O_h(i, j)))^2}. \tag{4.17}$$

Note from Eq. 4.14 that the overlap and the wasted area metric are purposely separated into two components so that they can be independently weighted. In most cases a single device will not be overlapped with more than 2 to 4 devices, while in those same scenarios, the devices with which it will attempt to get closer to are 11 to 13. So the overlap error component should be some times larger than the wasted area error to compensate for this issue and ensure that two devices are not being overlapped to reduce a placement's wasted area.

Cases where no overlap occurs between two devices should be accounted by the wasted area error, while cases where overlap does occur should be accounted by the overlap error. As such, two different distance metrics are defined from Eq. 4.17:

$$d^-(i, j) = O_b(i, j)d(i, j) \qquad (4.18)$$

and:

$$d^+(i, j) =! O_b(i, j)d(i, j), \qquad (4.19)$$

where $O_b(i, j) = (O_v(i, j) > 0) \& (O_h(i, j) > 0)$ (where & represents the logical *and* operation) represents a boolean that indicates whether devices i, j are overlapped and ! represents the logical *not* operation.

Using this minimum distance between pairs of devices, it is possible to evaluate a placement's wasted area through:

$$W_A = \frac{\sum_{i=1}^{N} \left(\sum_{j=1}^{N} \frac{d^+(i,j)}{N} \right)}{N \times \overline{w}} \qquad (4.20)$$

where N indicates the total number of devices in the topology and, $\overline{w}$ is the average width of the devices of the placement being considered and acts as a normalization factor. So the wasted area metric simply evaluates the average mean distance from which all devices are from each other.

Similarly, the overlap between can be calculated through:

$$O = \frac{\sum_{i=1}^{N} \left(\sum_{j=1}^{N} \frac{d^-(i,j)}{N} \right)}{N \times \overline{w}} \qquad (4.21)$$

where N indicates the total number of devices in the topology, $d^-(i, j)$ indicates the distance between devices i, j if there is overlap as defined in Eq. 4.18 and $\overline{w}$ is the average width of the devices of the placement being considered. So the overlap metric simply evaluates the average mean overlap distance (i.e. the minimum distance to solve an overlap scenario) between all devices.

4.3.2 Summed Symmetry Axis' Deviation

The symmetry axis of a pair of symmetric devices can be determined by calculating the centroid of the pair by first calculating the centroid of each individual device. This is defined by:

$$\dddot{x} = \frac{1}{2}\left(x_i + \frac{w_i}{2} + x_j + \frac{w_j}{2}\right), \tag{4.22}$$

where $\dddot{x}$ denotes the x coordinate of the pair's symmetry axis, $x_{i/j}$ the x coordinate of the bottom-left corner of device i/j and $w_{i/j}$ the width of device i/j. For self-symmetric devices $i = j$ and the equation holds true.

All of the devices' symmetry axis (if any exists) should have the same x coordinate, as such, the summed deviation of each pair's symmetry axis to any reference axis is given by:

$$\sigma_A = \sum_{k=1}^{M}(\dddot{x}_k - \dddot{x}_r)^2, \tag{4.23}$$

where M denotes the total number of symmetry groups in the circuit, $\dddot{x}_k$ the x coordinate of the k group's symmetry axis and $\dddot{x}_r, r \in [1, M]$ represents a reference axis either chosen randomly from any of the M existent or set as a parameter. For normalization purposes the layout is forced to be centered at $x = 0$ and so, all symmetry axis should be located at $x = 0$, therefore, taking as reference axis $\dddot{x}_r = 0$:

$$\sigma_A = \sum_{k=1}^{M} \dddot{x}_k^2 \tag{4.24}$$

where the value of $\dddot{x}_k$ is squared since it is easier to differentiate than the absolute value, thus facilitating the backpropagation of the error.

Additionally, symmetric devices should be located along the same horizontal line, that is, the y coordinate of both devices that constitute a symmetry group k should be the same. The difference in y coordinates between a pair of devices i, j that belong to symmetry group k is given by:

$$\Delta y_k^2 = (y_i - y_j)^2. \tag{4.25}$$

Similarly to what's done in (4.24), the difference between the y coordinates is squared to take into account the backpropagation phase. As such, the error associated to the deviation of the y coordinates between all the circuit's symmetric pairs is given by:

$$\sigma_y = \sum_{k=1}^{M} \Delta y_k^2. \tag{4.26}$$

Finally, symmetric pairs of devices should not have any overlap (note that this applies only to symmetry pairs and not to self-symmetric devices). Since the bottom y coordinates of both devices should be the same (therefore implying the existence of vertical overlap), for overlap not to occur, there should be no horizontal overlap. Since for the calculation of the symmetry axis' x coordinate in Eq. 4.22 it was necessary to calculate the center x coordinate of each device, it is efficient to calculate the horizontal overlap between two symmetric devices through:

$$\Delta x_k = max \left(0, \frac{w_i}{2} + \frac{w_j}{2} - \left| \left(x_i + \frac{w_i}{2} \right) - \left(x_j + \frac{w_j}{2} \right) \right| \right), \qquad (4.27)$$

where $\frac{w_i}{2} + \frac{w_j}{2}$ represents the minimum allowed x distance between the center of both devices and $x_{i/j} + \frac{w_{i/j}}{2}$ is the center x coordinate of device i/j. As such, error occurs if the distance between the center of both devices is smaller than the sum of their half widths, thus punishing any overlap. Note that the distance is not minimized, symmetric devices are not encouraged to be placed close to the symmetry axis since it might be beneficial for the placement to have another symmetry pair in between them in a $ABBA$ configuration. Additionally, it is clear that this error component is in many ways similar to the overlap error previously presented, however, the symmetry error should be self sufficient and not depend on the overlap error to solve symmetry issues. The error associated to the x distance between all of the circuit's symmetric pairs is given by:

$$\sigma_x = \sum_{k=1}^{M} \Delta x_k^2. \qquad (4.28)$$

Finally, the symmetry error is also normalized since a deviation of 5 nanometers can be significant if the device's layout width is 100 nanometers but not so much for cases where the average width is around 1 micrometer. However, the total layout's width is directly dependent on the prediction made by the network, so using it as a normalization parameter would cause erratic gradients and hinder the convergence process. As an alternative, the average width of all devices in the layout was used. The average width is also squared to match the symmetry axis' deviation units. The error is also normalized in relation to the total number of devices in the circuit since circuits with higher number of devices would have more devices contributing to the total symmetry axis' deviation resulting in a higher error. The final symmetry error is given by the expression:

$$S = \frac{\sigma_A + \sigma_y + \sigma_x}{N \times \overline{w}^2} \qquad (4.29)$$

where $\overline{w}$ denotes the average width of all devices and N the total number of devices in the circuit.

4.3.3 Current Flow Consistency Error

The direction through which the current flows, abstracting from the wiring between devices, can be determined by the sign of the difference in y coordinates between two consecutive devices in a current path. More specifically, between the top y coordinate of the first device and the bottom y coordinate of the second device.

Take the example of a placement solution in Fig. 4.10 for the SSA topology. one of the circuit's current paths is defined by [PM0, NM10] (current path number 0 in Table 4.2) that corresponds to [dev0, dev10] in the nomenclature used in Fig. 4.10. By calculating the direction of the current through the following equation:

$$C_D = sign(y_0^+ - y_{10}^-) \tag{4.30}$$

where $y_i^{+/-}$ denotes the top/bottom y coordinate of device i, it results in a current direction $C_D = 1$ (assuming the y coordinate is measured along the vertical axis, being 0 at the bottom of the layout limits and maximum at the top of the layout limits), meaning that in order for the layout to fulfill the current flow constraints, all current paths should be directed from top to bottom (also denominated as positive direction). Another current path is defined as [dev1, dev4, dev9] (can be seen in

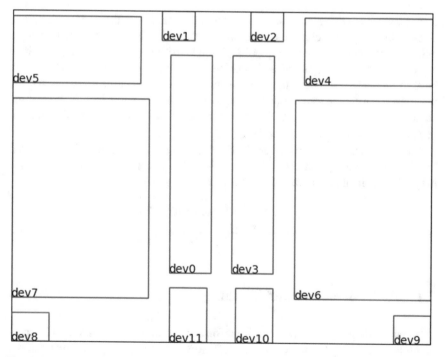

Fig. 4.10 Example of a placement for the SSA topology

Fig. 4.1), it is possible to confirm through the inspection of Fig. 4.10 that for all consecutive pair of devices, the top y coordinate of the first device is always greater than the bottom y coordinate of the second device, therefore, the current flows in a consistent manner and the associated error is null. As such, it is possible to quantify a layout's current flow consistency error through:

$$C_F = \sum_{i=1}^{n_{cf}} \sum_{\substack{j=1, \\ k=j+1}}^{d(CF_i)} -min(0, D_r(y_{ij}^+ - y_{ik}^-)) \tag{4.31}$$

where n_{cf} denotes the number of current paths in the circuit, $d(CF_i)$ the number of devices that make up current path number i, $y_{ij}^{+/-}$ the top/bottom y coordinate of the jth device in the current path i and D_r a reference direction, either chosen randomly from the ones existing in the suggested placement or set as a parameter.

In this work the current was forced to flow in the positive direction in order to avoid erratic gradients, through:

$$C_F = \sum_{i=1}^{n_{cf}} \sum_{\substack{j=1, \\ k=j+1}}^{devs(CF_i)} -min(0, y_{ij}^+ - y_{ik}^-). \tag{4.32}$$

Note that since in this model all currents are forced to flow in the positive direction, errors occur only if the current's direction is negative. If it is positive, then the error is null. This aspect is codified in Eq. (4.32) through $-min(0, y_j^+ - y_k^-)$ where positive current directions are ignored and negative directions are considered. These then have to be made positive so they contribute to an increase in the error that will be minimized during the training phase. It is also important to note that the greater the value of y_{ik}^- is in relation to y_{ij}^+, the greater the error, this is done so that the gradient of the error pushes y_{ik}^- to lower values.

Similarly to the symmetry error, the current flow consistency error is normalized in relation to both the number of devices N in the circuit and the average device height $\bar{h}$. The final normalized current flow error is given by:

$$C_F = \frac{\sum_{i=1}^{n_{cf}} \sum_{\substack{j=1, \\ k=j+1}}^{devs(CF_i)} -min(0, y_j^+ - y_k^-)}{N \times \bar{h}}. \tag{4.33}$$

4.4 Model Structure and Training

In order to compare the new model's performance with the one used in [12], most of the network's hyperparameters were left untouched to evaluate the impact of the changes made in the input vector and loss function. As such the model's structure and its hyperparameters are the following:

Table 4.7 Model's hyperparameters values

Hyperparameter	Value
Input Layer	480 features ($15 \times (2 \times 15 + 2)$)
Hidden Layers	4 Layers (2000, 750, 200, 100 nodes)
Output Layer	30 nodes (2×15)
Activation Function	ELU (Linear for the ouput layer)
Optimizer	Adam (α=0.001, β_1=0.9, β_2=0.999)
Regularizer	Dropout (drop rate=0.3)
Weights Initializer	Normal distribution
Loss Function	MSE, Topological Loss Function (equation 4.14)
Batch Size	500
Loss Function Weights	$w_a = 1, w_s = 400,$ $w_{cf} = 1 \times 10^{-3}, w_o = 700$

- The network's initial 3 hidden layers from [12] were not capable of codifying the data relation, as such, 4 hidden layers were used with 2000, 750, 250 and 100 nodes respectively were used;
- The activation function used in all nodes (except in the output layer's nodes that use a linear function) is the exponencial linear unit (ELU);
- Adam was left as the optimizer with the default values $\alpha = 0.001$, $\beta_1 = 0.9$ and $\beta_2 = 0.999$;
- Overfitting was addressed by using dropout in the hidden layers, using a dropping rate of 0.3;
- Initial random weights of the network layers were initialized by means of a normal distribution;
- Since the training dataset contains around 7000 to 14000 examples, the batch size was set to 500, which represents around 3.5% to 6.5% of the dataset, which is lower than the 10% threshold to be considered a big batch size;
- The topological loss function's (Eq. (4.14)) weights were empirically set to $w_a = 1$, $w_s = 400$, $w_{cf} = 1 \times 10^{-3}$ and $w_o = 700$. The weights were set in order to make all components similar in magnitude if the level of satisfaction is similar, e.g. for the placement in Fig. 4.8 one would expect a noticeably higher overlap error than symmetry error.

The model's hyperparameters are summarized in Table 4.7.

4.5   Conclusions

In this chapter, a thorough description of the proposed ANN model was given. In order to expand the scope of the solution, topology identifying features were added to input vector to distinguish between different topologies in the dataset. Additionally, these served, in conjugation with the introduced TLF, to focus the model's objective on producing any valid placement instead of following pre-defined guidelines. A topological constraint aware approach was used instead of the legacy layout based approaches in order to address the lack of innovation problem from [12]. The developed TLF attempts to explore the possibilities of the Supervised Learning by enabling the model to aim towards one between a variety of possible targets (any valid placement for a given sizing scenario). Finally, the ANN's functioning was taken into account when developing the constraint descriptive input vector through the use of appropriate categorical features encoding and scaling of the quantifiable ones, as well as during the development of the loss function, guaranteeing that it has no significant irregularities or plateaus.

Chapter 5
Results

In this chapter, different artificial neural network (ANN) models are tested and analyzed. They differ by the format of their input vector or by the loss function used during training, but the network's architecture is kept the same. The objective is to compare the impact of these isolated changes. All ANNs were implemented in Python language with TensorFlow [62] and Scikit-Learn [63].

5.1 MSE Models

Firstly, the models that use as loss function the mean squared error (MSE) equation (explained in-depth in Chap. 3 of this book) are explored. This section describes the structure of the networks and thoroughly analyzes the shortcomings of this approach, serving as a starting point to the development of the solution proposed on this book.

5.1.1 Structure and Training

Four variants of the MSE model were tested, these vary only in the structure of their input vector, which consist in variants of the *5-sizing* input vector structure used in [12], described in detail in Chap. 3 of this book and illustrated in Table 5.1:

- **Mean Squared Error—Non Polynomial Features (MSE-NP)**: The input vector is left unaltered (i.e., structure wise, each feature is normalized using standardization), that is, for each device its five sizing characteristics are stored and the

© The Author(s), under exclusive license to Springer Nature Switzerland AG 2020
A. Gusmão et al., *Analog IC Placement Generation via Neural Networks from Unlabeled Data*, SpringerBriefs in Applied Sciences and Technology, https://doi.org/10.1007/978-3-030-50061-0_5

Table 5.1 Device sizing info dataset used as input in [12]

Example #	Device 0					...	Device 11				
	w_0c	l_0c	nf_0	dw_0c	dh_0	...	w_11	l_11	nf_11	dw_0	dh_0
	(μm)	(μm)		(μm)	(μm)		(μm)	(μm)		(μm)	(μm)
0	17.5	0.36	3	3.48	8.07	...	8.7	0.89	3	4.73	5.14
1	17.7	0.36	7	6.52	4.765	...	83.3	0.83	7	9.47	14.4
...	...	...	...	...	...	...	...	...	...	...	...

input vector is formed through the successive concatenation of each device's characteristics. For all of the examples considered, the order of the devices was kept constant;

- **Mean Squared Error—Polynomial Features (MSE-P)**: For this model the order of the devices was kept constant as well, but polynomial features of degree 2 using only the crossed features were added, as explained in Chap. 2 of this book. The polynomial features were applied after the concatenation of each device's sizing characteristics, as such, features between devices were crossed as well;
- **Mean Squared Error—Non Polynomial Features with Device Scrambling (MSE-NPS)**: Similarly to MSE-NP, no polynomial features were used, but in this model the order of the devices is scrambled for every example in the dataset;
- **Mean Squared Error—Polynomial Features with Device Scrambling (MSE-PS)**: Finally, an MSE model is tested using both polynomial features and scrambling the order of the devices in each example.

Table 5.2 summarizes the differences between the variants as well as the length of the resulting input vector.

These models were trained with data from the single stage amplifier (SSA) circuit topology [60] only, since they were not prepared for multiple circuit topologies. As such, the target features consist in the x, y coordinates of the left-bottom corner of each device in the selected SSA template out of the 12 that were generated. In total, 10,422 sizing examples were considered, these were divided in three sets, a training set (70%), a validation set (15%) and a test set (15%). The model's hyperparameters are the ones defined in Table 5.3. Finally, each model was trained for 1,500 epochs.

Table 5.2 MSE models input vector structure variants

	MSE-NP	MSE-P	MSE-NPS	MSE-PS
Polynomial Features	No	Yes	No	Yes
Scrambled Device Order	No	No	Yes	Yes
Vector Length	$12 \times 5 = 60$	1831	60	1831

Table 5.3 Model's hyperparameters values

Hyperparameter	Value
Input Layer	480 features ($15 \times (2 \times 15 + 2)$)
Hidden Layers	4 Layers (2000, 750, 200, 100 nodes)
Output Layer	30 nodes (2×15)
Activation Function	ELU (Linear for the ouput layer)
Optimizer	Adam (α=0.001, β_1=0.9, β_2=0.999)
Regularizer	Dropout (drop rate=0.3)
Weights Initializer	Normal distribution
Loss Function	MSE, Topological Loss Function (equation 4.14)
Batch Size	500
Loss Function Weights	$w_a = 1$, $w_s = 400$, $w_{cf} = 1 \times 10^{-3}$, $w_o = 700$

5.1.2 Non-polynomial/Polynomial Features

The models without scrambling the devices' order are the ones that most faithfully follow the approach presented in [12]. Figure 5.1 shows the evolution of the average MSE error for the training and validation error throughout the 1,500 training epochs.

The analysis of both graphs shows that the MSE-P model further reduces the training error. But, it seems more prone to overfitting since the validation error increases as the model reduces the training error, suggesting a reduction in generalization.

To evaluate the model's capability of producing valid placements, the training and test outputs (after the training phase) of both models were tested using the topological loss function (TLF), explained in detail in Chap. 4 of this book, and defined as:

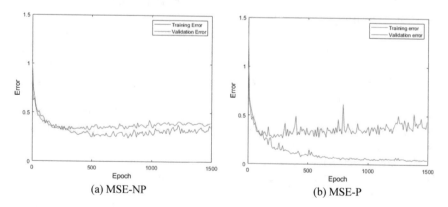

(a) MSE-NP   (b) MSE-P

Fig. 5.1 MSE models' without device scrambling training and validation error evolution. The error is evaluated using the MSE loss function

Table 5.4 Mean topological error of MSE-NP and MSE-P models

	Non-Polynomial		Polynomial	
	Training	Test	Training	Test
Wasted Area	1.61	1.44	1.68	1.59
Symmetry	1.22	1.42	1.74	2.37
Current Flow	0.00	0.00	0.12	5.24
Overlap	73.69	132.48	19.7	112.78
Total Error	76.52	135.34	23.24	121.98

$$loss = w_a W_A + w_s S + w_{cf} C_F + w_o O, \tag{5.1}$$

The average values for all the four factors that constitute the loss function as well as the total error are represented in Table 5.4. All of the values are already weighted using the values described in Table 5.3 and the total error is calculated using Eq. 5.1.

The results show, as expected, a higher topological error in the test sets when compared to the training sets. Also, the polynomial model presents a lower training error but its test error is comparable to its non-polynomial counterpart, further suggesting the occurrence of overfitting (early stopping and/or L1/2 regularization would certainly reduce this effect, as explained in Sect. 2.5 of this book, but the purpose of this comparison is to point out the model's tendency to overfit). Furthermore, a reduction in wasted area is generally accompanied by an increase in overlap error.

Note that overlap is also consistently the highest error component. To further understand this high test error, Fig. 5.2 represents a test prediction with approximately the mean error and the mean overlap error.

To further understand the possible causes for this test error, Table 5.5 contains information regarding the relative amount of times each of the 12 templates (that encode different and specific relative position between cells) was selected as target (i.e. the template that produced the layout with smallest area) for all of the 10,422 examples. Note that 91.33% of the examples are distributed among only four templates, in decreasing order of relevance: 5, 7, 9 and 4.

In order to ascertain the impacts of the unbalanced dataset, Fig. 5.3 shows how likely the model is of mistargeting an example given that it was targeted to a specific template. That is, the horizontal axis represents the template selected as target for any given example, the vertical axis represents the template closer (with minimum MSE) to the model's prediction. Each column is normalized in relation to the number of examples in each template. Therefore, the figure shows the probability of the model mistargeting to any of the templates y (vertical axis) given that the template selected as target is x (horizontal axis).

The largest values are located mainly in the main diagonal, which indicates that the model has correctly chosen to copy the target template. However, there are some clear exceptions in the training set, shown in Fig. 5.3a, such as the horizontal lines for template 7 and 4 that present high values throughout, meaning that the model is incorrectly basing its prediction in template 7 or 4. Also, columns for template 1 and

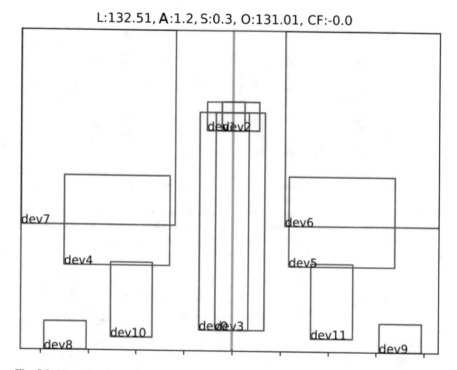

Fig. 5.2 Example of test placement solution for the MSE-NP model with the mean topological error

Table 5.5 Template selection rate for minimum area training

Template	0	1	2	3	4	5	6	7	8	9	10	11
Selection Rate (%)	2.76	0.48	5.35	0.00	18.04	25.84	0.00	25.53	0.01	21.92	0.06	0.00

10 show that they are significantly misclassified as others, especially considering the test set that has null values in the diagonal for these templates, which indicates they were never classified as themselves. This error is most likely a consequence of the imbalanced dataset as shown through Table 5.5. Figure 5.3b shows the same distribution but for the test set where lot of the examples are being mistargeted towards template 5.

The lack of a balanced dataset (that is not easy to produce) leads to a biased model that doesn't predict novel layouts, basing its predictions towards the most common templates across all examples. The change of the loss function to a topological evaluation of the prediction reduces the dependency on a balanced dataset and promotes the creation of novel layouts.

To further justify the change in loss function, Fig. 5.4a shows the distribution of the logarithmic average TLF error for each of the *(target template, most similar*

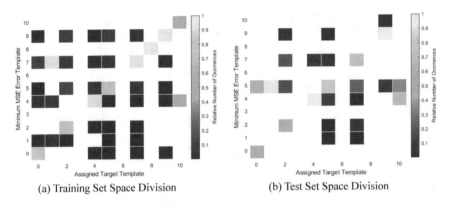

(a) Training Set Space Division   (b) Test Set Space Division

Fig. 5.3 Distribution of selected target template and the predictions' most similar template. Each column x is normalized so that the sum of the values for all y's is 1. White indicates no value because either the template was not selected for any example or because no examples with a given target template were ever mistargeted to a specific template

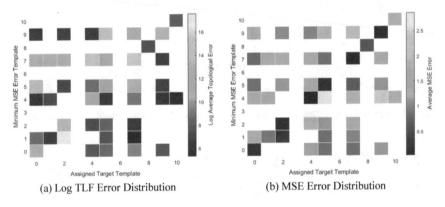

(a) Log TLF Error Distribution   (b) MSE Error Distribution

Fig. 5.4 Average error for given *target template/most similar template* pairs

template) combinations seen in Fig. 5.3. Similarly, Fig. 5.4b shows the distribution of the MSE error, this figure can be interpreted as how different template y is from template x.

As expected, the lowest MSE errors are located in the main diagonal, contrarily, for the TLF error, the main diagonal presents some relatively high values (e.g. the square with coordinates $(7, 7)$) and the lowest values are located in cases of mistargeting, as is the case of template 10 being mistargeted as template 4. In this particular example, template 10 is relatively similar to template 4 as Fig. 5.4b shows, presenting an average MSE error of around 1.5. However, note that when template 9 is mistargeted as template 4, it presents a relative low TLF error and high MSE error.

Figure 5.5 shows a prediction of the given scenario that presents low topological error and shows as well the difference between template 9 and 4. From this analysis it is possible to conclude that the MSE error doesn't appear to have any correlation

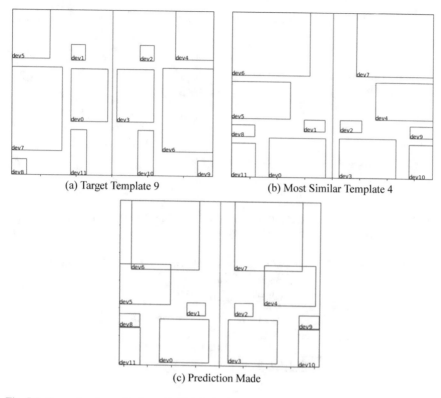

(a) Target Template 9   (b) Most Similar Template 4

(c) Prediction Made

Fig. 5.5 Example of a prediction with high MSE error but low TLF error

to the prediction's topological error, meaning that the quality of a prediction should be evaluated by a metric other than the MSE.

5.1.3   Device Scrambling

In order to discern the MSE models' ability to deal with circuit topologies never seen before, both MSE-NPS and MSE-PS models are trained with the order of the devices in the input vector scrambled.

The evolution of the training and validation loss for the two models are presented in Fig. 5.6. In both cases, the validation error is significantly higher than the training error (1.75 to 4 times higher), being higher than the validation error of both models show in Fig. 5.1 where the devices' order was kept constant. This discrepancy between the training and validation error shows that the model is unable to generalize the knowledge obtained during training due to the fact that there is no identifying feature for each device in the input vector.

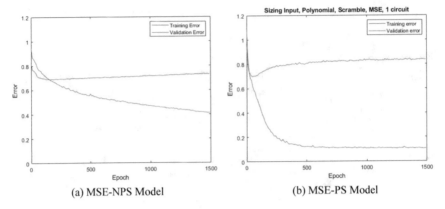

(a) MSE-NPS Model   (b) MSE-PS Model

Fig. 5.6 Evolution of training and validation error for an MSE model with sizing based input vector with the order of devices scrambled for each example

Table 5.6 Mean topological error of MSE models with scrambling of the device's order

	Non-Polynomial		Polynomial	
	Training	Test	Training	Test
Wasted Area	0.84	0.67	1.44	1.13
Symmetry	63.44	68.84	53.53	299.13
Current Flow	0.02	0.00	0.20	0.03
Overlap	386.92	568.18	100.40	265.65
Total Error	451.22	638.46	155.57	565.94

A template can be defined as a specific relative positioning of the devices adjusted to their sizing characteristics, for example, the template 9 shown in Fig. 5.5a is defined by having device 7 above device 8 but below device 5, however, if the order of the devices is scrambled, there is no way to distinguish between device 6 or 7, or even between device 7 and 0 since there are sizing examples where device 0 is larger than device 7. In a template, the reason why each device is located somewhere relative to any other is the result of the consideration of its topological constraints, hence, since in a sizing based input vector there is no reference to these constraints, it is impossible to distinguish between devices and thus the necessity of including in the input vector the topological constraints' description of each device.

Finally, the topological evaluation of the training and test predictions for both of these models is represented in Table 5.6. The overall error has consistently increased (at least 4 times) in each case when compared to the non-scrambled counterparts in Table 5.4.

Overall, the lack of the device's topological constraints' identifiers in the input vector hinders the detection of patterns to determine the relative positioning of each device.

5.2 Topological Models

The topological loss function (TLF) introduced in this work aims at solving the shortcomings of the previous models. In this section two different models that use the TLF as loss function are tested. One model is initialized through training 100 epochs using the MSE loss function and then switched to the TLF for 1,000 more epochs, and, the other model trained for 1,100 epochs using only the TLF. Additionally, both models use the constraint descriptive vector described in Chap. 4 of this book as input. The hypothesis also being tested here is the fact that the use of the MSE loss function in the early phases of training might speed up the convergence process and result in a better model.

5.2.1 Structure and Training

Both models are trained with a dataset composed by examples of the SSA and the cascode free single stage amplifier (CFSSA) [61] circuit topology, as such, the SSA examples' input vectors are padded and the order of the devices is scrambled for each example as explained in Chap. 4 of this book.

For the SSA topology, 10.422 different sizing cases are used while for the CFSSA circuit only 255 different sizing cases. However, to build a balanced dataset, each CFSSA sizing example is augmented 45 times changing the order of the devices in each copy totaling 11,475 total examples. The resulting dataset has a total of 21,897 examples that are split into a training (70%), validation (15%) and test set (15%).

For the MSE initialized model, during the training using the MSE function, the target placement used was automatically generated using a template based approach [3] that minimizes area without overlaps while upholding all symmetry and current flow constrains.

The rest of the models' parameters are described in Table 4.7 (including the TLF weights).

5.2.2 General Results

The evolution of the training and validation errors for both models is represented in Fig. 5.7.

The MSE initialization was introduced in order to initialize the model's weights in a stable region where the restrictions were closer to fulfilled, the TLF would then just make slight adjustments and optimize the results. The MSE initialized model achieves similar or even better results as can be noted in epoch 600 where its error seems to be smaller than the uninitialized model. To discern the influence of each

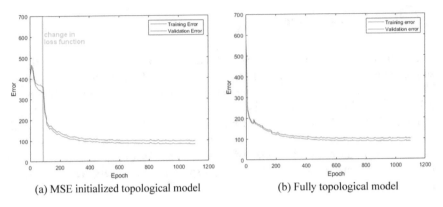

(a) MSE initialized topological model   (b) Fully topological model

Fig. 5.7 Topological models' training and validation Error Evolution. The error is evaluated using the TLF loss function

component in the total error, Fig. 5.8 shows the evolution of the individual error components over the training phase for the two topological models.

Note that the overlap error is the main component error in both models, and, while overlap and symmetry error can be easily analyzed, both the current flow and wasted area components are quite small in comparison and as such their evolution cannot be studied through Fig. 5.8.

To allow a better comparison between both models, the final average error for the training and test predictions for each model are shown in Table 5.7.

By analyzing Table 5.7 it is possible to conclude that the difference between the test and training errors is not as significant as for the MSE models. For the MSE models without device scrambling (the results shown in Table 5.4), the test error is 76% and 425% higher than the training error without polynomial features and with polynomial features, respectively. For the topological evaluation based models, the test error is only about 20% higher in both cases. So even though the training error is larger for the topological evaluation based models, there is a clear improvement in the generalization of the knowledge gained. Note in Fig. 5.7 the similarity between the shapes of the validation and the training curves in both cases, it seems that whenever the model reduces the error for the training set, the effect of the update on the network's weights is equally felt in the validation set, this further corroborates the hypothesis that the generalization of this model is higher when compared to its MSE counterparts. Note also in Table 5.7 that the MSE initialized model has a considerable lower current flow error, this being the only clear advantage of the model over its fully topological counterpart.

In order to interpret the errors of Table 5.7 further, Figs. 5.9 and 5.10 show the best, the worst and the three quartile test predictions for each of the models, on top of each prediction there is a description of its error components.

By analyzing the predictions made, Table 5.7 and the evolution of the distinct error components in Fig. 5.8, it is clear that the main difficulty of the model is avoiding overlap between devices, clearly representing the majority of the error. In matter

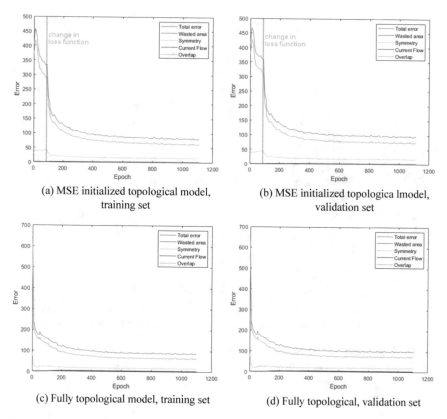

Fig. 5.8 TLF error components' evolution throughout training. The error is evaluated using the TLF loss function

Table 5.7 Mean topological error of topological models

	MSE Initialized		Topological	
	Training	Test	Training	Test
Wasted Area	2.75	2.65	2.98	2.85
Symmetry	15.40	18.46	15.58	17.70
Current Flow	0.66	0.71	4.02	4.40
Overlap	63.74	77.28	63.36	74.77
Total Error	82.55	99.1	85.94	99.72

of fact, the high overlap weight is so that overlap minimization is prioritized over the other error components through its higher gradient. Note that even for the worst predictions, the model seems capable of properly interpreting both symmetry and current flow constraints.

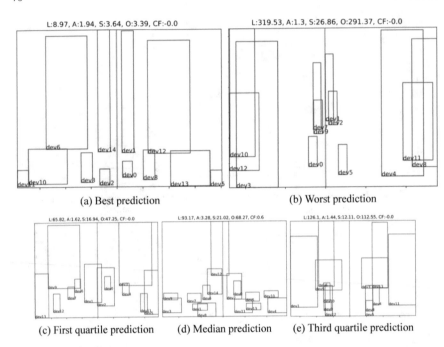

Fig. 5.9 Sampling of the fully topological model's test predictions. The weighted error components of each prediction as well as the total loss value are printed on top of each figure

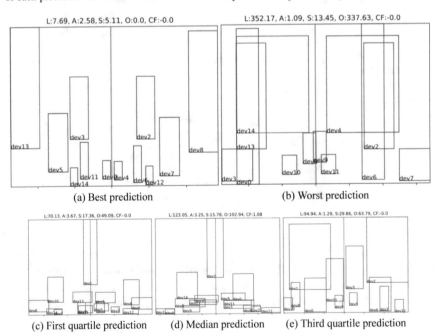

Fig. 5.10 Sampling of the MSE initialized topological model's test predictions. The weighted error components of each prediction as well as the total loss value are printed on top of each figure

5.2.3 TLF Components Correlation Analysis

One question that should be posed now is *what's the influence of each component on any of the others*? For example, it is intuitive that an increase in the prediction's wasted area should lead to a decrease in the overlap between the devices, however, the relation between the current flow error and symmetry (if any) is harder to visualize. To address this question, an analysis on the correlation between the components for both models was made (for the MSE initialized model, the correlation was studied once the model had been initialized and the training using the TLF began). The study was made using Pearson's correlation coefficient. Figure 5.11 shows the results of the analysis.

As expected, there is a strong negative correlation between wasted area and overlap, with a coefficient of $\rho = -0.9$ for the MSE initialized model and $\rho = -0.8$ for the uninitialized one. Note that in every case, the coefficients are not as pronounced for the uninitialized model, however, the signs are consistent across both examples, which strengthens the credibility of the most pronounced results. The already examined overlap/wasted area (O_L / W_A) correlation for example, presents high negative values in both cases meaning that most likely there is a somewhat strong negative correlation between both even if not as strong as the results in Fig. 5.11a might suggest. Other significant examples are the pairs current flow/wasted area (C_F / W_A), symmetry/overlap (Sym / O_L) and Sym / W_A. Note that in every case the registered p-values meet the criteria $p < 0.001$ meaning the correlations are statistically significant.

The pair C_F / W_A presents high positive correlation between the two, meaning that an increase in wasted area (which translates in an increase of the prediction's area) is met with an increase in current flow error, this correlation can be explained through the analysis of the current flow error's definition:

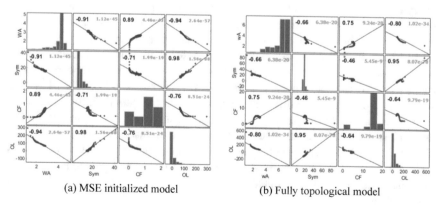

(a) MSE initialized model   (b) Fully topological model

Fig. 5.11 Pearson correlation analysis between the components of the TLF. The p-values for each pair are shown in green. For the MSE initialized model, the analysis was made for the samples after the change in loss function

$$C_F = \sum_{i=1}^{n_{cf}} \sum_{\substack{j=1, \\ k=j+1}}^{devs(CF_i)} -min(0, y_{ij}^+ - y_{ik}^-), \tag{5.2}$$

where n_{cf} denotes the number of current paths in the circuit, $devs(CF_i)$ the number of devices that constitute the current path number i, $y_{ij}^{+/-}$ the top/bottom y coordinate of the jth device in the current path i.

The equation reflects that if two devices are in the incorrect order, e.g. device A is above device B when it should be below, the error is higher if B maintains its position and A is moved further above (i.e., in the wrong direction). This means that for a given prediction with a pair of devices in the wrong order, if the layout is simply expanded outwards maintaining the relative position of each device, its current flow error increases. In the same manner, once the layout is shrunken, the current flow error decreases. Note that if originally the two devices were already in the correct order, the error would remain 0 once the layout was expanded, thus, an increase in wasted area can only lead to either the increase in current flow error or its stagnation, which can clearly be seen in the scatter plot of both components in Fig. 5.11a.

There is a strong negative correlation between the pair Sym/W_A meaning that an increase in area is followed by a decrease in symmetry error, this relation can be explained when taking into account the high weight associated to the overlap error and the nature of the symmetry between devices. Symmetry between any two devices is fulfilled if their symmetry axis is centered in $x = 0$ and their y coordinates are the same, this presents a fragile equilibrium where both devices have to be placed taking the other into consideration, as such, finding the perfect symmetric placement is a result of small corrections on each of the involved device's positioning. These small corrections, when made in a compact layout, may increase significantly the overlap error, as such, these corrections are discouraged by the overlap component's high gradient, so once the layout is expanded these corrections can be made and the symmetry error decreases. This also explains the existing positive correlation between the pair Sym/O_L since a decrease/increase in overlap error (increase/decrease in wasted area) is followed by a decrease/increase in symmetry error. If the hypothesis made is true, it should be possible to verify these relations in the evolution of the error components, however, due to the different scale of the error components, these cannot be easily compared in Fig. 5.8. In order to visualize these influences, Fig. 5.12 shows the evolution of the different components for the uninitialized model, each normalized using *minmax* normalization (explained in Sect. 2.8) so they are all in the same scale. The figure corroborates the supposition made as the area of the predictions increase in order to reduce the other error components. There is however a noticeable jump in the current flow error at around 100 epochs, which is not easily explainable, as no other component suffers such drastic changes that could explain this behavior.

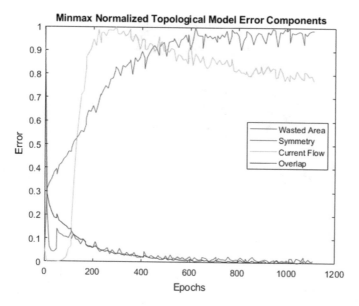

Fig. 5.12 Normalized, through *minmax* error components' evolution during training for the fully topological model

5.2.4 Test Dataset Augmentation

Since the topological models are robust to the order of the devices in the input vector, each sizing example can be theoretically augmented $15! \sim 1.3 \times 10^{12}$ times by changing the order of the devices in each copy produced. As the purpose of this work is to develop a push-button speed model capable of producing a valid placement solution for a given sizing example, it could be part of the system's flow to first augment the given example by changing the order of devices before passing these through the model. In practice, as long as one of these augmented vectors produces a valid placement, the objective is fulfilled. As such, in this subsection, each example in the test set of the fully topological model is augmented and a placement solution is generated for it, the best of which is selected as final placement solution.

In order to fulfill the desired push-button speed, each example was augmented 100 times. To make sure the desired speed is still met, a test was run to compare the time it took to make a single prediction and 100 predictions. A single prediction took 0.0304 s while 100 predictions took 0.0396 s. This slight increase in time is considered within satisfactory bounds.

The mean topological errors for the augmented test set, and, comparison with the not augmented test and training sets are represented in Table 5.8.

There is a significant reduction in error, particularly in the overlap component that is even lower than the training set error. To best compare the results, the predictions were sampled similarly to what's seen in Fig. 5.9. The results are shown in Fig. 5.13

Table 5.8 Mean topological error of fully topological model with test set augmentation ($\times 100$)

	Topological		Augmented
	Training	Test	Test Set
Wasted Area	2.98	2.85	3.39
Symmetry	15.58	17.70	11.12
Current Flow	4.02	4.40	1.09
Overlap	63.36	74.77	11.04
Total Error	85.94	99.72	26.65

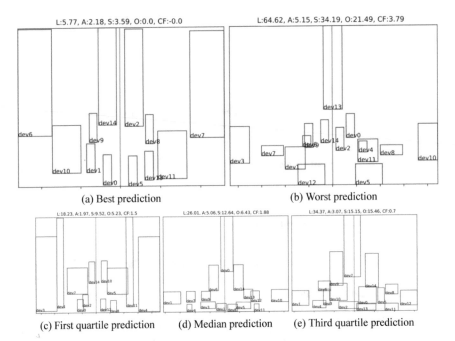

(a) Best prediction   (b) Worst prediction

(c) First quartile prediction   (d) Median prediction   (e) Third quartile prediction

Fig. 5.13 Sampling of the topological model's augmented test set predictions. The weighted error components of each prediction as well as the total loss value are printed on top of each figure

and the difference in quality is clear when compared to Fig. 5.9. With the augmented test set, the worst prediction in Fig. 5.13b is better than the first quartile prediction from Fig. 5.9c.

5.2.5 Generation of Novel Layouts

In order to test the fully topological model's capability of producing novel layouts, two sizing scenarios were picked at random from the test dataset, one of the SSA topology and one of the CFSSA topology. Each of these two was augmented (with the

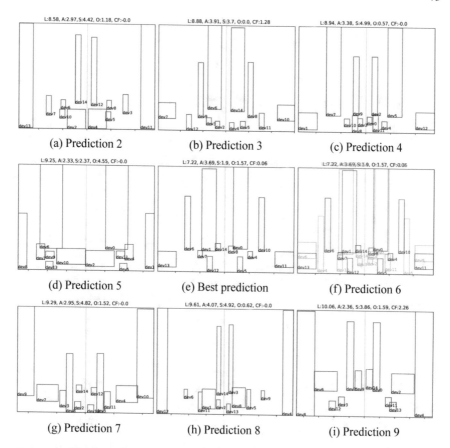

Fig. 5.14 9 different predictions for a single sizing case of the SSA topology after 1000 scrambled copies of the same example were tested

order of devices scrambled) 1000 times and predictions were generated for each copy. Out of all the predictions, the 9 with least error are chosen as suggested placements. If the model is capable of producing novel layouts, these 9 should be considerably different from each other. Figures 5.14 and 5.15 show the results for the SSA and CFSSA examples respectively.

The results in Fig. 5.14 show a noticeable difference between predictions and it is safe to say a variety of placements are suggested. The predictions in Fig. 5.15 however, show more similarity between them. This might be due to the fact that the increasing number of devices limits the amount of possible placements. Another possibility might be the lack of different sizing cases for the CFSSA topology in the training set. Different sizing cases are the only cause for innovation when considering only one topology since these may lead to overlapping, and thus, the model is forced to correct these overlaps by searching for a different relative positioning of the devices. As such, the lack of sizing cases may lead to the formulation of a more general

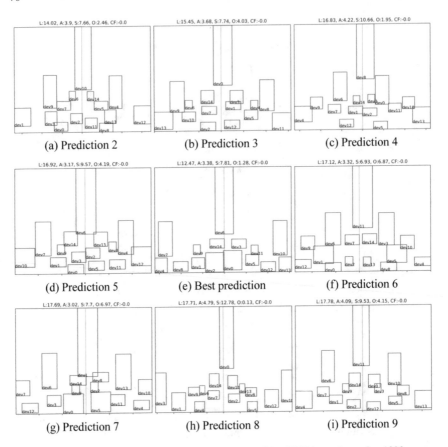

Fig. 5.15 9 different predictions for a single sizing case of the CFSSA topology after 1000 scrambled copies of the same example were tested

placement that worked for all the sizing cases in the training data, making test data be targeted towards the same placement (i.e., the same relative device positioning). Note that in Fig. 5.14 all predictions have the same sizing characteristics, it means that templates are being attributed to the order of the devices, which is beneficial for the application since it makes results like these and the ones discussed in Sect. 5.2.4 possible.

Finally, to enforce the strict fulfillment of the constraints, the predictions made can be easily post-processed through a simple symmetry enforcing and compacting algorithm. The algorithm starts by fixing the minor mismatches in symmetric pairs by placing them at their average y coordinate and, keeping their distance between one another fixed, shifting their symmetry axis to match the reference axis. After, the y coordinates of all devices are doubled, thus doubling the y separation of all devices, after which the x coordinate can be more easily compacted avoiding overlaps (this is done using an interval tree). Finally, the y coordinates are also compacted using an

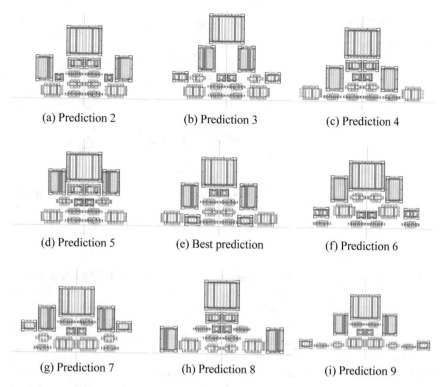

(a) Prediction 2   (b) Prediction 3   (c) Prediction 4

(d) Prediction 5   (e) Best prediction   (f) Prediction 6

(g) Prediction 7   (h) Prediction 8   (i) Prediction 9

Fig. 5.16 Post-processed top 9 CFSSA predictions for a single sizing scenario

interval tree. The whole process of prediction generation and post-processing took 40 ms. The post-processed compact placements for the top 9 CFSSA placements are presented in Fig. 5.16.

It is clear that this simple post-processing step has not only successfully corrected the minor symmetry mismatches as it produced more compact placements at a slight computational cost. Note that this fast optimization is only so effective due to the quality of the initial placement. If symmetry mismatches or overlaps were more noticeable, a costlier process would have to be used.

5.2.6 Folded Single Stage Amplifier Circuit Test

In order to test the model's performance with a new circuit that was not seen by the model during training, the folded single stage amplifier (FSSA) is introduced. Its schematics is presented in Fig. 5.17 with the current paths superimposed.

In order to convert the circuit into an input vector, both its symmetry and current flow constraints should be properly encoded. The circuit is composed by 14 devices,

Fig. 5.17 Folded Single
Stage Amplifier: schematic
with current paths
highlighted

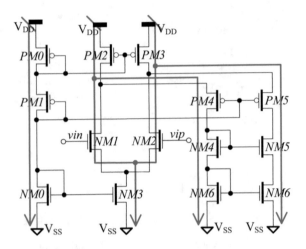

which is less than the 15 used in training so the input vector will be padded with an empty device descriptive vector. Note that the circuit is composed by four different self-symmetric devices that represents a novelty to the network, as this pattern was not found in the training data.

One single sizing case was augmented 1,000 times by scrambling the order of the devices in each example, then, similarly to what was done in Sect. 5.2.5, the 9 predictions with smaller error were selected as final output. Table 5.9 shows the mean loss and its weighted components for the top 9 predictions while these can be visualized in Fig. 5.18.

Although the mean loss value for these 9 predictions is quite high when comparing to previous case studies using TLF, it is still comparable to the test set topological errors for the MSE-NP and MSE-P models shown in Table 5.4. However, note that the FSSA circuit topology introduces 4 different self-symmetric devices. Up until

Table 5.9 Mean topological error of the top 9 folded circuit predictions (Out of 1,000)

Wasted Area	Symmetry	Current Flow	Overlap	Total
1.55	50.34	0.32	110.57	162.78

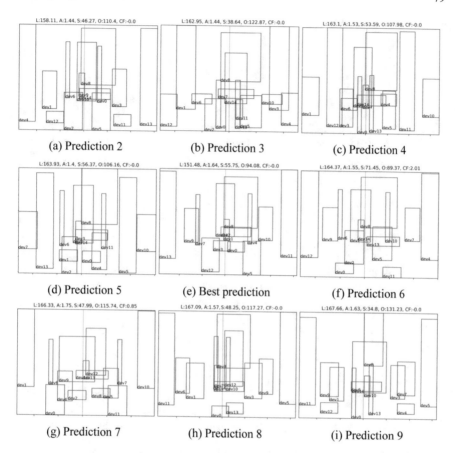

Fig. 5.18 9 different predictions for a single sizing case of the FSSA topology after 1,000 scrambled copies of the same example were tested

this point the model had only ever dealt with one single self-symmetric device and has learned to deal with it accordingly, by placing it in the top center of the layout (top due to the current flow constraints). By applying this simple logic to the new topology, all four self-symmetric devices are placed in the top center of the layout resulting in a big overlap between these devices as it can be seen in all of the 9 predictions. Note that this at least means that the model is capable of recognizing self-symmetric devices. In order to better evaluate the predictions made, Fig. 5.19 shows the same predictions but without the self-symmetric devices. While there is

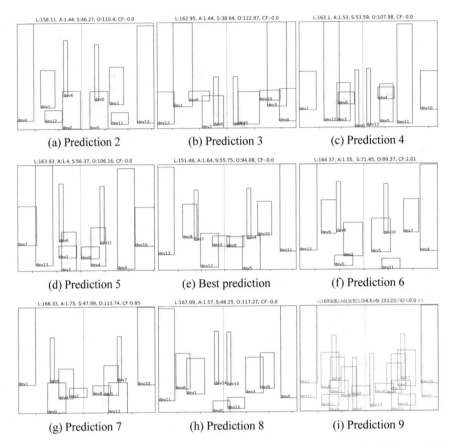

Fig. 5.19 9 different predictions for a single sizing case of the FSSA topology after 1000 scrambled copies of the same example were tested

still some significant overlap, it is clear that symmetric pairs were clearly identified. Note as well that the current flow error is quite minimal in all predictions.

Overall the model seems to have correctly identified the topological constraints of the circuit and seems to have attempted to satisfy them using the methods that it had learned before.

5.3   Conclusions

In this chapter, the two general approaches of MSE and TLF based models were compared. TLF based models have shown a greater generalization performance, being able to achieve test losses very similar to the training ones, meaning all the knowledge that was being acquired during training was also applicable to the test set.

The TLF only model was even able to achieve some interesting results with a circuit topology never seen before, however the gained knowledge was not enough to deal with such an alien scenario of four self-symmetric devices. As such, it is important to subject the network to an even greater variety of relevant patterns during training, or even just provide some greater variability of patterns. For example, if the training set had examples with two and three self-symmetric devices, the variability would prevent the network to deal with self-symmetric devices in the same manner, placing them in the center and top. This would force the network to deal with these scenarios in a more generalizing way since no simple rule would result in all scenarios.

Chapter 6
Conclusions and Future Work

6.1 Conclusions

In the work described in this book, a new approach to use artificial neural networks (ANNs) towards automatic analog integrated circuit (IC) placement was tested. The introduction of a loss function that evaluates the quality of a prediction based on the fulfillment of multiple considered topological constraints allowed the generation of novel placements solutions tailor made for each example, as well as eliminating the need for the pre-production of tested legacy layouts. The distinction between different circuit topologies was made possible through the constraint descriptive vector used as the input vector that together with the input vector padding enabled the introduction of multiple circuit topologies using the same model. The device-level constraint identification and satisfaction approach resulted in a greater generalization of the acquired knowledge as the model correctly identified constraints in never seen before topologies. The use of ANNs is suited to the problem as it enabled the production of solutions at push-button speed as well as being especially good at detecting patterns in input/output pairs, which were then generalized to the surrounding input space.

The current results still do not present the necessary performance for real world application as too many invalid layouts are still being produced. It is clear however, that the results are promising, having a better performance than previous approaches. As such, the proposed methodology and models serve as a proof of concept for this novel approach and clearly entices further optimization and research.

6.2 Future Work

This work served mainly as proof of concept for the implementations done in the input vector and loss function, as such, the necessary focus was never given to the tuning of the hyperparameters, which constitutes a pivotal part on the optimization

© The Author(s), under exclusive license to Springer Nature Switzerland AG 2020
A. Gusmão et al., *Analog IC Placement Generation via Neural Networks from Unlabeled Data*, SpringerBriefs in Applied Sciences and Technology,
https://doi.org/10.1007/978-3-030-50061-0_6

of any ANN model. The tuning of these parameters may not only lead directly to better performance but might also optimize the learning process enabling the use of more training examples that should certainly lead to better results. One of these hyperparameters are the loss function's weights that were set through trial and error, for optimal results some grid search on the parameter's space (with the use of cross-validation to faithfully compare models) should have been performed, however this would take an immense time with the available machines. Note even that other regression models like random forest might have been tested and explored to solve this problem.

An augmentation of the training set could be done in two different manners: considering the use of the same topologies, each example in the training set could be augmented by creating copies of it with the order of the devices scrambled; or, new circuit topologies with never seen before constraints could easily be introduced, due to the fact that the used loss function doesn't require the production of target placements, input vectors could be artificially mass generated to create a vast training set. However, these input vectors should have only relevant sizing solutions and feasible constraints, where an example of an unfeasible constraint would be a device symmetric to two others or contradictory current flow constraints. If these feasible constraints are properly codified, then an in-depth and efficient search of the feature space would be possible.

The encoding of each constraint in the input vector could be further researched as well, more efficient representations would result in smaller input space and further optimization of the learning process. Additionally, cross features such as each device's area or dimensions' ratio could reduce the predictions' error, especially the overlap component.

One of the greatest challenges in creating a model capable of multiple topology layout generation is that when larger topologies (composed by more devices) are considered, the expansion of the input space may hinder the learning process especially for smaller topologies, as such, Recurrent Neural Networks may prove an interesting alternative as each device would successively be placed into the layout considering the devices that had already been placed before.

References

1. International Technology Roadmap for Semiconductors (ITRS) 2012 edition, http://public.itrs.net/
2. N. Lourenço, R. Martins, N. Horta, *Automatic Analog IC Sizing and Optimization Constrained with PVT Corners and Layout Effects* (Springer, Berlin, 2017)
3. R. Martins, N. Lourenço, N. Horta, *Analog Integrated Circuit Design Automation-Placement, Routing and Parasitic Extraction Techniques* (Springer, Berlin, 2017)
4. G.G.E. Gielen, R.A. Rutenbar, *Computer-aided design of analog and mixed-signal integrated circuits* (Proc, IEEE, 2000)
5. R. Martins, N. Lourenço, N. Horta, *Generating Analog IC Layouts with LAYGEN II, Book in the series SpringerBriefs in Applied Sciences and Technology* (Springer, Berlin, 2013)
6. E. Afacan, G. Berkol, A.E. Pusane, G. Dündar, F. Başkaya, A hybrid Quasi Monte Carlo method for yield aware analog circuit sizing tool, in *Design, Automation and Test in Europe Conference and Exhibition (DATE)* (2015)
7. R. Martins et al., Many-Objective Sizing Optimization of a Class-C/D VCO for Ultralow-Power IoT and UltralowPhase-Noise Cellular Applications. IEEE Trans. VLSI Syst. **27**(1), 69–82 (2019)
8. I. Abel, M. Neuner, H. Graeb, Constraint-programmed initial sizing of analog operational amplifiers, in *IEEE 37th International Conference on Computer Design (ICCD)* (2019)
9. M.P.-H. Lin, Y.-W. Chang, C.-M. Hung, Recent research development and new challenges in analog layout synthesis, in *21st Asia and South Pacific Design Automation Conference (ASP-DAC)* (2016)
10. R. Martins, R. Povoa, N. Lourenço, N. Horta, Current-flow and current-density-aware multi-objective optimization of analog IC placement. Integration **55**, 295–306 (2016)
11. B. Prautsch, U. Hatnik, U. Eichler, J. Lienig, Template-driven analog layout generators for improved technology independence, in *16th GMM/ITG-Symposium on ANALOG 2018* (2018)
12. D. Guerra et al., *Artificial neural networks as an alternative for automatic analog IC placement, in 16th International Conference on Synthesis* (Modeling, Analysis and Simulation Methods and Applications to Circuit Design (SMACD), 2019)
13. M.I. Jordan, T.M. Mitchell, Machine learning: trends, perspectives, and prospects. Science **349**(6245), 255–260 (2015)
14. P. Domingos, A few useful things to know about machine learning. Commun. ACM **55**(10), 78–87 (2012)
15. H. Wang, J. Yang, H.-S. Lee, S. Han, Learning to design circuits (2018)

© The Author(s), under exclusive license to Springer Nature Switzerland AG 2020
A. Gusmão et al., *Analog IC Placement Generation via Neural Networks from Unlabeled Data*, SpringerBriefs in Applied Sciences and Technology,
https://doi.org/10.1007/978-3-030-50061-0

16. N. Lourenço, E. Afacan, R. Martins, F. Passos, A. Canelas, R. Póvoa, N. Horta, G. Dundar, *Using polynomial regression and artificial neural networks for reusable analog ic sizing, in International Conference on Synthesis* (Modeling, Analysis and Simulation Methods and Applications to Circuit Design (SMACD), 2019)

17. K. Zhu, M. Liu, Y. Lin, B. Xu, S. Li, X. Tang, N. Sun, D. Pan, GeniusRoute: a new analog routing paradigm using generative neural network guidance (2019), pp. 1–8. https://doi.org/10.1109/ICCAD45719.2019.8942164

18. B. Xu, Y. Lin, X. Tang, S. Li, L. Shen, N. Sun, D.Z. Pan, Wellgan: Generative-adversarial-network-guidedwell generation for analog/mixed-signal circuit layout, in *56th ACM/IEEE Design Automation Conference (DAC)* (2019)

19. F. Bre, J.M. Gimenez, V.D. Fachinotti, Prediction of wind pressure coefficients on building surfaces using artificial neural networks. Energy Build (2018)

20. A. Cauchy, *Méthode générale pour la résolution des systemes d'équations simultanées* (Comp. Rend. Sci, Paris, 1847)

21. B.T. Polyak, *Some methods of speeding up the convergence of iteration methods* (USSR Comput. Math. Math, Phys, 1964)

22. N. Qian, On the momentum term in gradient descent learning algorithms. Neural Netw (1999)

23. S. Ruder, An overview of gradient descent optimization algorithms (2016)

24. J. Duchi, E. Hazan, Y. Singer, Adaptive subgradient methods for online learning and stochastic optimization. J. Mach. Learn. Res. (2011)

25. D. Kingma, J. Ba, Adam: a method for stochastic optimization (2014)

26. D.E. Rumelhart, G.E. Hinton, R.J. Williams, Learning representations by back-propagating errors. Nature (1986)

27. Sci-Kit Learn, Underfitting vs. Overfitting, https://scikit-learn.org/stable/auto_examples/model_selection/plot_underfitting_overfitting.html

28. J. Depois, Memorizing is not learning! (2019). https://hackernoon.com/memorizing-is-not-learning-6-tricks-to-prevent-overfitting-in-machine-learning-820b091dc42

29. A. Amidi, S. Amidi, Deep learning tips and tricks cheatsheet, https://stanford.edu/~shervine/teaching/cs-230/cheatsheet-deep-learning-tips-and-tricks

30. I. Goodfellow, Y. Bengio, A. Courville, *Deep Learning* (MIT Press, Cambridge, 2016)

31. N. Srivastava, G. Hinton, A. Krizhevsky, I. Sutskever, R. Salakhutdinov, Dropout: a simple way to prevent neural networks from overfitting. J. Mach. Learn. Res. (2014)

32. G.-B. Huang, Learning capability and storage capacity of two-hidden-layer feedforward networks. IEEE Trans. Neural Netw. (2003)

33. J. Ke, X. Liu, Empirical analysis of optimal hidden neurons in neural network modeling for stock prediction, in *IEEE Pacific-Asia Workshop on Computational Intelligence and Industrial Application* (2008)

34. S. Trenn, Multilayer perceptrons: approximation order and necessary number of hidden units. IEEE Trans. Neural Netw. (2008)

35. B. Xu, N. Wang, T. Chen, M. Li, Empirical evaluation of rectified activations in convolutional network (2015)

36. D.-A. Clevert, T. Unterthiner, S. Hochreiter, Fast and accurate deep network learning by exponential linear units (ELUs) (2015)

37. C. Nugent, California Housing Prices-Median house prices for California districts derived from the 1990 census (2017). https://www.kaggle.com/camnugent/california-housing-prices

38. K. Pearson, On lines and planes of closest fit to systems of points in space. The London, Edinburgh, and Dublin Philosophical Magazine and Journal of Science (1901)

39. K. Potdar, S. Taher, D. Chinmay, *A comparative study of categorical variable encoding techniques for neural network classifiers* (Int. J. Comput, Appl, 2017)

40. A. Von Eye, C. Clifford, *Categorical Variables in Developmental Research: Methods of Analysis* (Elsevier, Amsterdam, 1996)

41. P.-H. Lin, Y.-W. Chang, S.-C. Lin, *Analog Placement Based on Symmetry-Island Formulation* (IEEE Trans. Comput.-Aided Des. Integr, Circuits Syst, 2009)

42. M.J.M. Pelgrom, A.C.J. Duinmaijer, A.P.G. Welbers, *Matching properties of MOS transistors* (IEEE J, Solid-State Circuits, 1989)

43. A. Hastings, *The Art of Analog Layout* (Prentice Hall, Upper Saddle River, 2006)

44. H. Graeb, F. Balasa, R. Castro-Lopez, Y.-W. Chang, F.V. Fernandez, P.H. Lin, M. Strasser, Analog layout synthesis–Recent advances in topological approaches, in *Design, Automation and Test in Europe Conference and Exhibition* (2009)

45. S. Nakatake, Structured placement with topological regularity evaluation, in *Asia and South Pacific Design Automation Conference* (2007)

46. C.-W. Lin, J.-M. Lin, C.-P. Huang, S.-J. Chang, Performance-driven analog placement considering boundary constraint, in *Proceedings of the 47th Design Automation Conference on–DAC* (2010)

47. R. Martins, N. Lourenço, N. Horta, *Analog Integrated Circuit Design Automation* (Springer, Berlin, 2017)

48. R. Martins, N. Lourenço, A. Canelas, N. Horta, Stochastic-based placement template generator for analog IC layout-aware synthesis. Integration (2017)

49. R. Martins, N. Lourenço, N. Horta, *Multi-objective optimization of analog integrated circuit placement hierarchy in absolute coordinates* (Expert Syst, Appl, 2015)

50. L. Zhang, R. Raut, Y. Jiang, U. Kleine, *Placement algorithm in analog-layout designs* (IEEE Trans. Comput.-Aided Design Integr, Circuits Syst, 2006)

51. S.C. Maruvada, A. Berkman, K. Krishnamoorthy, F. Balasa, Deterministic skip lists in analog topological placement, in *6th International Conference on ASIC* (2005)

52. Y.-C. Chang, Y.-W. Chang, G.-M. Wu, S.-W. Wu, B*-trees: a new representation for non-slicing floorplans, in *Proceedings of the 37th ACM/IEEE Design Automation Conference (DAC)* (2000)

53. P.-N. Guo, C.-K. Cheng, T. Yoshimura, An O-tree representation of non-slicing floorplan and its applications, in *Proceedings 1999 Design Automation Conference* (1999)

54. J.M. Cohn, D.J. Garrod, R.A. Rutenbar, L.R. Carley, *KOAN/ANAGRAM II: new tools for device-level analog placement and routing* (IEEE J, Solid-State Circuits, 1991)

55. Y.-P. Weng, H.-M. Chen, T.-C. Chen, P.-C. Pan, C.-H. Chen, W.-Z. Chen, Fast analog layout prototyping for nanometer design migration, in *2011 IEEE/ACM International Conference on Computer-Aided Design (ICCAD)* (2011)

56. R. Martins et al., Two-Step RF IC block synthesis with pre-optimized inductors and full layout generation in-the-loop. IEEE Trans. Comput.-Aided Design Integr. Circuits Syst. **38**, 989–1002 (2019)

57. S. Bhattacharya, N. Jangkrajarng, C.-J. Shi, *Multilevel symmetry-constraint generation for retargeting large analog layouts* (IEEE Trans. Comput.-Aided Design Integr, Circuits Syst, 2006)

58. P.-H. Wu, M.P.-H. Lin, T.-C. Chen, C.-F. Yeh, X. Li, T.-Y. Ho, A novel analog physical synthesis methodology integrating existent design expertise. IEEE Trans. Comput.-Aided Design Integr. Circuits Syst. **34**(2), 199–212 (2015)

59. A. Gibbons, *Algorithmic Graph Theory* (Cambridge University Press, Cambridge, 1985), p. 5

60. R. Povoa, N. Lourenço, R. Martins, A. Canelas, N. Horta, J. Goes, Single-stage amplifier biased by voltage combiners with gain and energy-efficiency enhancement, express briefs. IEEE Trans. Circuits Syst. **II**, (2018)

61. R. Povoa, N. Lourenco, R. Martins, A. Canelas, N. Horta, J. Goes, A folded voltage-combiners biased amplifier for low voltage and high energy-efficiency applications, express briefs. IEEE Trans. Circuits Syst. **II**, (2020)

62. M. Abadi et al., TensorFlow: large-scale machine learning on heterogeneous systems. Software available from https://www.tensorflow.org/ (2015)

63. F. Pedregosa et al., Scikit-learn: Machine Learning in Python. J. Mach. Learn. Res. (2011)